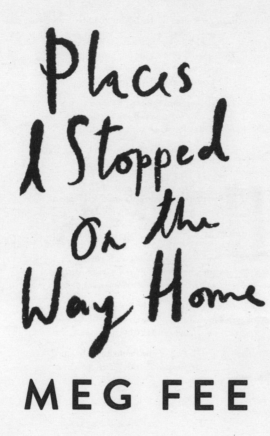

MEG FEE

ICON

First published in the UK in 2018
by Icon Books Ltd, Omnibus Business Centre,
39–41 North Road, London N7 9DP
email: info@iconbooks.com
www.iconbooks.com

This edition published in the UK in 2019 by Icon Books Ltd

Sold in the UK, Europe and Asia
by Faber & Faber Ltd, Bloomsbury House,
74–77 Great Russell Street,
London WC1B 3DA or their agents

Distributed in the UK, Europe and Asia
by Grantham Book Services,
Trent Road, Grantham NG31 7XQ

Distributed in the USA
by Publishers Group West,
1700 Fourth Street, Berkeley, CA 94710

Distributed in Australia and New Zealand
by Allen & Unwin Pty Ltd,
PO Box 8500, 83 Alexander Street,
Crows Nest, NSW 2065

Distributed in South Africa
by Jonathan Ball, Office B4, The District,
41 Sir Lowry Road, Woodstock 7925

Distributed in India by Penguin Books India,
7th Floor, Infinity Tower – C, DLF Cyber City,
Gurgaon 122002, Haryana

Distributed in Canada by Publishers Group Canada,
76 Stafford Street, Unit 300
Toronto, Ontario M6J 2S1

ISBN: 978-178578-451-4

Typeset in Mrs Eaves by Marie Doherty

Printed and bound in Great Britain
by Clays Ltd, Elcograf S.p.A.

This work reflects the personal experiences and perspectives of the author; while she has tried to tell her story truthfully, some names and descriptions have been changed to protect the identity of others.

For my parents, who did the bravest thing parents can do and let me fail.

"These are the days that must happen to you."

WALT WHITMAN, "SONG OF THE OPEN ROAD"

CONTENTS

FOREWORD

Before Meg Fee was my friend, I was a fan. Of course, I still am. I read Meg's blog—found solace in her corner of the internet—in the loneliest hour of my twenties, comforted and buoyed that there was somebody else out there, my age, in a big city, with wild and determined and oh-so-trusting conviction that there's love to be had that will last a lifetime.

As we've crossed into our thirties together and blog reading turned to email turned to visits in cities the world over, I still turn to her and her wisdom for guidance. She's a realistic romantic, a practical dreamer. It's the levelheaded hopefulness that gets me. She had me at "I believe." She had me at "I deserve."

When I learned the title for this collection, a collection years in the making, in both living and writing, it stole the breath from my belly. Meg's understanding of home, her articulation and pursuit of it, has pushed me to keep on the path—no matter how many times I, too, stop off on the way.

We talk about it a lot, Meg and I. About doing the work and getting dirt under the fingernails in the trenches of real life, about hanging out in the room of love. Being love itself. Meg holds me accountable to myself—to being my rawest, most authentic, honest and kind version—through her example. When I first discovered her words I felt that too: that by definition of being privy to her journey, and the everyday courage it takes to keep putting one foot in front of the other, I was implicated. Because she shared her story, I was inherently tasked as her reader with treating my own with the same loving scrutiny. What's remarkable is that Meg has made me feel like not only can I do this, but I must.

"I am every man who has hurt me, and the quiet hope that we've only got to get it right once," Meg writes in this collection of essays, and I rather think that's it. We've only got to get love right once. And if Meg has taught me anything (she has taught me everything) it's that every single last thing else is in service of that one. And so, we carry on. Dented and willing and worthy and very much ourselves.

Just as she does.

Laura Jane Williams
London, 2018

DISCLAIMER

This is a love letter to the nights I climbed into bed with a full face of makeup, too tired to take it off. To the days when one latte was not enough, when the two basic food groups were caffeine and sugar. This is a note to the girl I was when joy was a thing always ten feet away, when getting out of bed was harder than not. This is an open-mouthed sloppy kiss to the city that changed me, to the years that gathered in quick succession, to the men who were not right, and to the girlfriends who kept me afloat. This is a note to the nights I got home at five in the morning, lips stained, chin red and raw, happy. This is a missive both to and from the muddled middle. An ode to the mess and grace that is growing up. And a thank you to the girl I was at twenty who knew that, hard as things were, her life was changing and if she could bear witness to it—stay awake enough to sit with it—then she could transform the most heartbreaking moments of her life into the most meaningful. This is my bent and broken and wholly imperfect version of what happened and how it happened. And this is my declaration that, given the chance, I wouldn't change a thing.

THE WEST VILLAGE

Many years ago I found myself in a tiny, dimly lit restaurant in the West Village drinking red wine with the playwright Sam Shepard.

It was a year before I graduated from Juilliard with a Bachelor of Fine Arts in Drama, a few more before I learned that red wine always leaves me on the bathroom floor, and more still before I'd come to understand that writing would be the love of my life.

It was 2007 and Mr. Shepard was at Juilliard to receive an honorary doctorate. I was his escort for the day, which basically meant it was my job to make sure he wore the robe and hood correctly and didn't wander off on his own. The ceremony passed as expected and was followed by a champagne cocktail reception in the President's suite—the same place the Rolling Stones had kicked off their world tour two years before; Juilliard was a mostly odd and wondrous place. The administration had warned us that none of the honorees would likely stick around for the event, but on this occasion, everyone seemed game for a party. Which is how I found myself sitting next to the pre-eminent American playwright talking about things I now mostly can't remember.

At the start of the reception I stood at one end of the room, drink in hand, shifting back and forth on my feet. I badly wanted to speak to Mr. Shepard but was too afraid to approach him. Despite my being the person charged to look after him for the day we'd said no more than five words to one another, and it was clear that he was deeply skeptical as to why I was there. Another student, a guy I didn't know terribly well, came and stood next to me. He watched as I squirmed, and listened as I mumbled something about *Famous playwright* and *What must he think* and *Should I say something*, and this boy half-laughing said, *If you want to talk to him, all you have to do is walk over there.* How simple, how easy, how very much like jumping off a cliff! But courage requires first a decision, and then a leap. And so in a moment of rare grit I walked across the room and sat next to him. I laugh now because it is almost always in this way that good things happen—one person walks towards another—a small, seemingly unimpressive act that gives way to better things.

The cocktail hour lasted several more, and when it was nearly done Mr. Shepard turned to me and asked if I'd like to attend an event that evening—it wasn't a big thing, he was going to be introducing a film he'd written many years before. *Yes*, I said, another leap. And so, hours later, I sat in the basement of the Rubin Museum on 18th Street. The guy at the front desk had let me in without asking for either my name or a ticket— New York is a tremendous place to be both young and a woman. I found an open seat, and a few minutes later Mr. Shepard stood at the front of the stage and read aloud from his screenplay of the film *Paris, Texas*. And then, just as the movie began, he took a seat, a single beer on the table in front of him. Twenty minutes into the film, when he pushed back his chair, I took a breath and followed him out. We nearly bumped into one another on the street. *I didn't think you'd come*, he said smiling. *I know, I'm sorry, but here I am*, I replied, a quiet laugh born of nerves and something ever so slightly sturdier than fear. *Have you seen the film? Do you want to go back in*, he asked? *No, I'll watch it another time*, I said. Which is how I came to spend a night in my early twenties drinking red wine in the West Village with one of the greatest American playwrights.

This is what I remember: Amy Winehouse played on the radio. We talked about horses, his farm in Kentucky, and his not being terribly keen on New York. And when we walked down the street he placed the palm of his hand against the back of my neck in a way that I have spent every day since hoping another man will do without me having to ask. When the night ended, he kindly walked me to the subway, and we never saw each other again.

What everyone wanted to know right after, as I attempted to describe the event of my *pseudo-date with Famed American Playwright, Sam Shepard*, was if he spoke about writing—he was notoriously private about such things. And the thing is, he did. I'm quite sure he did.

My only hesitation is that, through the muck and fuzz of red wine and a time in my life that I don't remember terribly well, might I just have imagined the next part? He spoke of his love of music and how what he really wanted to do was be a musician—a rocker—but because he didn't know how, or couldn't, he wrote plays. And writing, just as he did, was his attempt at music.

★

After I was accepted to Juilliard I visited the college with both of my parents. It was April and snowing. We sat with the administrative director and asked the expected questions and, when it came time for a tour, I asked to go alone. My father now describes this day—and this moment in particular—as one of the saddest of his life. I can't help but wonder if something in him could sense all the heartache that would happen in that building on 66th Street, or if it was simply that I was leaving—that I was doing what he and my mother had raised me to do: to chart my own course, willfully and without fear. After the visit, when it became clear that there would be no reasoning with me about bachelor's degrees from other fine universities, a deal was struck. I'd be allowed to attend but under one condition: I was to keep a journal. No one would read it; rather its purpose was to continue to exercise that part of my brain that liked to write. It would serve as a sort of renegade education to develop a different set of muscles. How prescient that now seems.

I moved to New York the following August, eighteen years old, so sure of my future. I was dating Colin, a man six years my senior. We had met the month before, working at a summer camp in Florida, and had been pushed together by friends. He was tall and lanky and bright, but not my guy, which I knew right away. But I was so unsure of how love was meant to go that I thought, *Well okay, maybe*, and ignored the small tug of the gut that said, *Nope, not this.* And I'd nearly convinced myself that it could work, until I visited Colin's apartment for the first time and he handed me a single key. As I closed my hand around it, all I could think was, *I don't want this.*

Sitting on the floor of his living room one night, eating pecan ice cream, we looked through his pictures and vinyl records, and I felt totally unprepared for the intimacy of learning about this man's life. He put Ella Fitzgerald on the record player and hummed along. I flicked through the photos and scribbled notes, trying to reconcile the young boy smiling at the camera with the man sitting next to me.

Who is your Ella? he asked.

What? I said, looking up, startled.

Who is your Ella? he asked again.

I didn't understand the question and said so.

What is the music you most love—the music that undoes you?

I didn't yet have the life experience to understand the question, let alone answer it. *Oh. I don't know*, I said quietly, returning to the photos in front of me.

I can't wait for you to find out, he said, smiling at me. *The finding out is the best part.*

I broke up with him not long after, a month after arriving in New York, at a small table next to a large window in a cheap diner on the corner of 68th and Broadway. He was too far ahead of me—those six years between us too loaded and full. Already he had the answers to so many questions I had yet to even ask. "Time After Time" played on the radio as we sat there, a plate of fries between us, mostly untouched.

Maybe if we'd met at another time, I said, trying to cushion two words: "not you."

Don't do that. Don't lie to make this easier, he replied.

At the 66th Street subway station we hugged uncomfortably and he disappeared down the steps, the city seeming to rise up and swallow him whole in that moment. I turned away and walked up the steps towards college, the air suddenly cooler, sweeter; fall coming in fast and hard.

Colin was a valuable lesson in listening to that voice that says, *Not this.* I don't think of him often, but when I do, I think of the question he asked as we sat on the floor of his apartment that night. *Who is your Ella?* Which is to say, what do you love? What has meaning for you? What fills you with joy?

The thing is, he was right: the finding out is the best part. In my early twenties I mapped New York by its small concert venues. The Bowery Ballroom on

Delancey Street. Mercury Lounge on the corner of Houston and Essex. Rockwood Music Hall on Allen. Standing in those dark spaces, people pushing in from every side, I found "Ella" in the broken voices of Charlie Fink and Kristian Matsson. I found her in the vulnerability with which Laura Marling sings and Johnny Flynn plays the fiddle. I found her in lyrics that called upon Bukowski and Shakespeare. In songs that stirred those low unknowable, unnamable parts of myself, and that upon listening granted a perfect moment in which I stood just as still as I could because someone else had given voice and melody to what I thought singular and secret.

But it was more than that. I found Ella as I sat on too-long subway rides furiously scribbling notes in the margins of books. "Ella" became not a question of who, but what. And the answer, fundamentally, was language—words written and spoken and sung. Language, endlessly malleable, and frighteningly insufficient and still human.

I graduated from Juilliard in 2008 just as the economy plummeted, and I began to write as a way to stave off and sort through a personal sadness. Writing felt like wrangling storm clouds, which is to say, impossible. But so did life. Writing became a way to make peace with that which was flawed. The writer Jack Gilbert began his poem "The Forgotten Dialect of the Heart" with "How astonishing it is that language can almost mean, and frightening that it does not quite."[1] Writing became an exercise in sitting with discomfort, accepting that which is imperfect, and reveling in the *almost*.

The thirteen years since Colin first asked that question have been almost entirely in service of finding Ella, and my place in New York, and myself, too.

I may never be able to fully say what this swath of time took from me, nor what it gave in return, but I know that it made me, shaped me—gave with both hands but took even more.

And Mr. Shepard was right, too. Arranging words is much like making music. Flawed and small and still with a beat and a pattern and the capacity to empty the air from one's lungs.

Like him, I can't write music and I sure as hell can't make it. But everything I've written here is my best attempt at it. My graceless offerings that I lay at the altar of Art. Small essays made up of imperfect words that *almost* mean—my own humanity made manifest.

THE A TRAIN

I cling to Will's dark leather jacket as he leans against the subway pole, one finger nestled into the deep V of his zipper. I am eighteen years old and four months into this new life in New York. Everything feels like an invitation. I don't yet know the A train—don't know where it will go or how it will get there—only that he knows, that he will lead, and I will continue to cling.

LINCOLN CENTER

I have three photos from college that I keep together. They were all taken on the same night, in the span of five minutes, in a room that was warm in that way a room gets when everyone is drinking and dancing and celebrating the end of something really big.

In the first photo I'm sandwiched between two boys, and there's a girl to the left of us whose name I now can't remember.

The camera was on the wrong setting: two lines streak across the frame. Three of us are staring at the lens, all smiles, but for Will to my left, his lips against my cheek, his light brown hair barely visible beneath his baseball cap, a serious look on his face.

In the second photo, it's just the two of us. I'm looking into the lens, and he, in full profile, with that strong jawline and those clear green eyes, is staring straight at me. I laughed good and hard as all this was happening, both endlessly tickled and wildly frustrated. *Can you please just look at the camera?* I begged. *Can I just have one photo of the two of us together?*

I don't remember his response—what he said or if he smiled—but the third is the two of us, our cheeks pressed together, looking straight ahead. *Click.*

I was eighteen when I first met Will. It was an afternoon in late August, my first week of college. I was sitting on a red couch in the first-floor lobby waiting to check my email, as we were all still years away from having access on our phones. He caught my eye and grinned from under his cap as he logged off and turned around. He had a smile that felt exceptionally generous. I remember wondering in that moment if we had already met, if he was also a drama student? We were properly introduced a few weeks later and struck up an easy friendship. He was in his fourth and final year and had these kind, light eyes that would crinkle ever so slightly as he laughed, his shoulders lifting in amusement. We fit in hasty conversations between classes, extended tentative invitations, took late-night strolls after cheap pizza and too much beer, hanging back behind the others, his hands casually finding their way to my waist, quickly dropping if anyone turned around.

It was at a party on 123rd Street, pretty early into that first year that I watched as he emerged from the bathroom with another girl trailing just behind. I was standing in the hallway, waiting in line, when the door opened. He glanced at me as he passed, his eyes quickly finding the floor. She had dark brown hair that fell to her waist. Her lips were stained a deep plum and she wore a bright yellow dress that hung loose on her dancer's body. To this day she is one of the most beautiful women I have ever beheld. But her eyes were red and swollen in that way that reveals heartbreak, and I knew immediately I'd just seen a thing that would make everything else—everything after—harder. When the night ended, with his hand gripping the bit of my leg just above my knee, I pushed the thought of her out of my mind.

I was sitting with my back against a row of lockers the first time he kissed me. It was November and the sky was that particular blue-gray that hangs low on the city for the better part of four months. Will emerged from a classroom dressed in sweats and socks. He paused and leant over me, his lips a shock of cool and wet against my forehead. It was as gentle a thing as could be. I had always imagined our first kiss would be a sort of delicious collision: messy and imperfect and totally thrilling. But what I actually got was something altogether better.

I fell in love with him on a Sunday afternoon at the start of December, both of us lying on the couch, my head on his chest, the music of Nick Drake playing softly in the background. I had taken the subway home with him after a party in Chelsea the night before where we played foosball and drank cheap wine. Early into the evening he invited me up to the roof with him. I panicked—afraid and certain of what we were so clearly moving towards. How odd our wants are—how strange it is that fear and desire live together, a mottled border between. *It's closed off right now*, someone said. *No one can get up there.*

Just after midnight, when he casually invited me home, I looked him right in the eye and said *yes*. We took the subway some 150 blocks north and played video games, and at one of those impossible hours between midnight and morning he offered me pajamas and a bed in the next room over; his roommate was away for the weekend. Instead I took his hand, and followed him into his bedroom. I was so young, but so sure.

It was a stolen half of a weekend. The next morning, in that cavernous apartment off of the last stop on the A train, with its exposed brick on the east-facing wall, his bedside table piled high with books and plays, we watched *Rushmore* and *Winged Migration*, and he pulled out a disk with the one scene he'd filmed before college. We didn't actually sleep together that night—but everything I learned about intimacy was learned in that bedroom in an apartment on 207th Street.

I loved him the way you can only love someone the first go round: foolishly—and silently. Because that's what happens when you fall in love with a man who is in love with someone somewhere else. He never said as much, but I knew. It's not that it was a secret, we just didn't talk about it. And as long as we didn't say it, as long as we talked over and around it, we could pretend. Will called me "trouble" one night, and I didn't really understand what that meant—the full weight of it. "Inconvenient," by another name. Not long after, we sat on opposite ends of the same couch and he told me it couldn't continue as it had, and I said it couldn't continue at all, and he smiled, his eyes full with apology. *You never know*, he said, *it might all work out.* But she moved to New York the following spring, and I spent the rest of the year treading water, pretending I was fine.

Three years later, at the start of my last year at Juilliard, Will and I sat across from one another in a small Thai restaurant just west of the Theatre District. He was two years out of college and we'd barely spoken in the time since—a few phone calls at most, and never at the important moments. I was so sad, depression stretching like a wasteland in all directions. I did my best to smile—to give the impression of a girl who bats her eyelashes easily, but the added weight of my body belied my many secrets. When he spoke to me about the sadness of the previous year—how success doesn't protect against despair—I held my tongue because I didn't know how to say that I'd nearly forgotten what joy felt like. Instead I said, *Maybe happiness is a choice* (it isn't), and he said, *Love— love, too. We choose who we love.* And I sat there, heartbroken, because for the life of me I couldn't figure out how to un-choose this person, or why he was saying this to me. He proposed to his girlfriend a few months later.

★

Eight years after first meeting, Will and I made love on a white couch, on the ground floor of the house of a person I'd never met, deep into a part of Tribeca I'll probably never be able to afford. He was staying with a friend who was away for the weekend, and he pulled out a Sam Shepard film for us to watch, teasing me about the glass of wine I'd shared with him. The film took place on a farm and I made some joke about chickens, and he laughed, throwing his head back, the skin around his eyes buckling in deference to joy, and I thought heaven must be making a man laugh whenever you want. Just as the movie got going, he pulled me into him, pushing my navy dress to the side—the one I wore when my body felt large and unmanageable—and we did what we hadn't done all those years before.

I couldn't sleep that night, so I turned to my side, my head on his shoulder. I studied the outline of his face, his strong nose, how his hair, now grayer than before, spilled in all directions. I got up in the middle of the night to use the bathroom and when I returned to bed I found Will's arm thrown out to the space where I'd just been. No one prepares you for that. For a man's awareness of your absence. He pulled me into him without ever waking, pressing his nose and mouth into the side of my face, and I lay there without moving, trying not to breathe, wondering how he could.

At breakfast the next morning he asked about happiness, his eyes on the eggs in front of him, his marriage having ended some months before. We were at a posh restaurant in the Meatpacking District—one of those places people say you simply must go when visiting New York. The girl who seated us wore red lipstick and a pillbox hat; the waiter spoke with a heavy French accent. We sat outside at a table too small, our knees touching below. No one recognized him then; how different that would be now. My dress tugged at my neck, and a tree in bloom loosed flowers into our food. I told him that I made my bed every morning and kept a clean apartment and drank more lattes than a person reasonably should, and that those things seemed as good a way as any to swim to the dry land that is happiness. *Yes*, he said, *but did you do it on your own?* And I knew if I answered honestly—*alone*—it would be years before we'd meet again, if ever. When the waiter took our plates the food was mostly untouched.

From time to time now I'll pass a newsstand and see Will smiling on the front of some glossy magazine, his face so handsome—the gray in his hair charming, the ever-deepening lines around his eyes flattering. But I pause just long enough to see beyond what age and money have made of him. I look to find the boy I rode the A train with when New York was new and more promising than not, before sadness took hold and upended it all. I look to find the man who spent that first year smiling up at me from under a Twin Cities baseball cap, his face then softer, his eyes alight with something wild. I look to find the guy I fell in love with before I knew that love stories aren't always linear and that sometimes you don't get the guy.

★

The three photos I have from the end of my first year are not high quality. The lighting is wonky and the images grainy and I am tired in all three—a certain roundness having settled onto my face that would go on to define the next stretch of years. But God am I glad to have them. Because they answer so many questions. Because when I look at those photos I remember that on a night late into the May of my first year at Juilliard, a man I loved looked at me like I was magic, and I have the pictures to prove it.

66TH STREET

I lose my period immediately. My breasts, soon after. I am nineteen years old, halfway through my first year of college, and systematically chipping away at the curves of my body, unconsciously attempting to empty myself of something far more pressing—sadness, which is to say, life, in all of its complexity.

I am hungry all the time, a pain tucked high and pulsing just under my lowest left rib, and I wonder if this feeling will last forever.

I remember little of this time, except that I am heartbroken and newly ashamed of my desire and sexuality, both so messy and so human, both so suddenly exposed. I am out of my depth. I am a woman, and I don't want to be. Hunger seems preferable to sadness, and so I cling to it.

If I cannot change the fact that one man does not—or cannot—love me, then I will change my body. I will make the intangible tangible. And then I won't feel so lonely. And then New York won't feel so large. And then everything will be easy. And then and then and then, ad infinitum. I am not foolish enough to think *And then Will will love me*, rather the feeling is: *And then it won't matter*.

I stand in front of a mirror and study my body. I

know I have gained weight—the scale tells me so, but I cannot see it; I never was tremendously skilled at seeing gradations in women's bodies, least of all my own. But I stand in front of the mirror and I change the way I define what I already see: *Not thin anymore, fat.* Four words, five minutes, and a bit of a rewire to the brain. *Fat now.*

Fat to be lost, a new body to chase—a better one. And with that, an easier life, surely.

I begin to build a life predicated on the notion of *and then*, which means life is always somewhere just beyond my reach. And the ultimate *and then*, the one I cannot admit to myself, is one of worth. I will become thin, and then I will be worthy.

Life is reduced to a series of lists. Of what I have eaten and what I will eat. Of what I want to eat and what I cannot. Of all that I will do once I am thin and everything I imagine I will be. Of the version of myself so different than the one who stands in front of the mirror and cannot bear to exist within her physical form.

And I am reduced to a body, growing ever smaller, ever less like a woman. Yet I am also aware of some silent indoctrination, some invisible threshold that I have crossed: that to hate my body is to join the ranks of women everywhere.

The first day of the diet is the last day of my period until many months after I begin to eat more. I do not know that I am starving myself, am only told after. I am following a diet recommended by both my pediatrician and gynecologist, and I am doing it exactly as prescribed—I am as close to perfect as I have ever been. I delight in the stunning clarity of the boundaries, the set number of calories, and each week I am rewarded as I stand on the scale, physically less than I was the week before, never mind that the questions of who I am and what I want are growing ever less voluble.

The thing is, starvation isn't just the absence of food—it is also the absence of enough food. I am eating, but not enough. A starving body has evolved over many millennia to seek out food and store it as fat. This is an immutable truth.

And so the hunger comes for me, and there is no end to it, there is only more hunger. Hunger is physical, of course, but it is many other things besides: a longing to take up space, to want, to need, to fall in love, to establish boundaries, to say *not good enough* or *not this* or *not now*, to change directions, to start again, to fail, to forgive, to be uncompromisingly human.

The pounds pile on and with them a tremendous sadness, a desperate panic that I have failed. A fear that because I am unable to wrangle this most basic human need I am somehow *less than*. Not as good, not as worthwhile. I am human, flawed and imperfect, which is, of course, all I ever was and all I was ever going to be. It is unbearable.

I spend the bulk of my twenties in the trenches of a really severe eating disorder, and while it is definitely about my body, it is also about things messier, more complicated, and less clear. There is a time my parents and I gauge my weight like some sort of barometer of happiness. And the act of that makes us crazy because, although inextricably bound and ridiculously tied, their association was never so straightforward.

★

I got out of a very dark hole with nothing but desire and my fingernails. I clawed my way to a better life with grit and a wish between my teeth.

All these years later and I am still surprised by my breasts. Slightly bewildered by how round and full they are. Shocked by the gentle slopes of my body. Secretly delighted by the mutable flesh. Humanity made manifest.

So much of what I now know and understand I learned from that very peculiar disease. Food became both a metaphor and microcosm for how to deal with the larger world. A friend once said to me, *Food isn't always meant to be enjoyed. Sometimes you have to eat the thing that doesn't taste that great because it is really, really good for you.* I think of that often. Sometimes you have to do the thing you really don't want to do because it is really, really good for you—and by good I mean vital and necessary and capable of inching one's life forward. I learned that it is my job to show up, to sit with discomfort. To face the seemingly impossible.

I believe in eating cherries in the summer and cheese whenever. I believe a calorie is a nearly worthless measure of a food's value, and no one needs a scale in their bathroom. I believe in avocados when they're in season and wine in the evenings. Cheeseburgers and pizza and hot dogs at four in the morning after a night out. Full fat lattes, always, and champagne when so inclined.

Occasionally I still feel a pain in my chest, high behind my left rib. It is duller than hunger, but just as important. It is joy and sadness and the sweet terror of a persistent loneliness. It is the fear that nothing will change and the faith that of course it has to. It is the ache of my own humanity. And it is the best, and truest, thing about me.

UPPER WEST SIDE

I wear a navy, scalloped skirt on our first date. And makeup—eye makeup, concealer, even, which will be a great comfort to my mother. I'm quite sure I even brush my hair, a far cry from those first six months of college when I didn't own a hairbrush. I am so nervous—excitement abutting terror.

I meet Patrick at a time when need surpasses desire. I am newly 24, just a year and a half out of college, and New York is knee-deep in a winter that shows no signs of ever ending. I am sad in a way that is overwhelming and ever-present, untraceable to neither person nor thing.

I enter the restaurant on West 67th, just off of Columbus and ask the girl at the desk if anyone is waiting; she nods in the direction of the U-shaped bar just behind her.

We had met only two nights before, at a French restaurant in the West Village. I almost didn't go. That's what I remember. That earlier in the evening I'd felt low and blue, and so nearly sent a message to the friend organizing it: *Next time*. I don't know what small force got me there, but I entered the restaurant and walked to the end of the bar to join those I recognized. I noticed

Pat, but didn't know if he was part of our group. And then I felt his eyes on me. We sat at a large table in the middle of the dining room, about ten of us altogether, celebrating a friend's birthday. Pat wore glasses, his hair neatly shorn. He angled to sit next to me, and I let him. He spent the evening suggesting dates and places to go and things to do, and I smiled and laughed, emboldened by his attention. But when the dinner ended and he shuffled his feet, unable to actually ask for anything, I scribbled my number on a slip of paper and tucked it into the pocket of his jacket, clinging to the life raft of his affection.

Two nights later, I stand at the entrance of a restaurant, relieved I am able to pick him from a crowd. Pat is at the bar, so relaxed, nearly handsome.

The first time I find myself in his apartment, I run my fingers over his books. So many books, stacked ceiling to floor. He points to some framed prints in the entryway when we walk in—*Very expensive, very famous*, he says while demanding I tell no one. But I am more interested in the many books just to the right of the fireplace. I stop at one of my favorites, my fingers lingering on the familiar spine.

This one, here, I say, tapping it and turning around to look at him, *I loved this one.*

I didn't like it, he says, glancing over from where he lies on the floor, before closing his eyes and ending the conversation.

Later I will wonder if I should have known at this moment.

But before I come to know, I think *maybe*. And Pat thinks *maybe*. And together we live in that delicious and fertile place that a *maybe* is—until we find ourselves on opposite sides of the same answer: *No. Absolutely not.* And there in the wake of the said-and-done will be the exposed mettle of a man who is just not good enough. But for so long I confuse his not good enough with my not good enough and that becomes the story I tell myself. *That I am not good enough.*

We never make love. I'm not ready, and then he doesn't want to. The closest we get is late one night at the start of March when he asks me to undress. I peel off my tights and pull at the zipper on my skirt, and he comments on all the many layers I use to conceal my body. He knows, of course; I had come right out and told him once after he remarked how he'd never seen me wear a pair of jeans. How to explain? The straightest line is usually the truth. And so I had given him mine in the best and clearest way I knew how. *I'm not entirely well; my body mostly doesn't feel like my own.* He teased me about this— immediately—and I laughed, because in that moment it felt nice—normal, even.

But on this night he tells me to remove my top—my bra, too—and lie naked, pressing my breasts hard into his back as I massage his neck. *At least this way I'll feel like I got something,* he says. Ten words. Silently, I climb onto his bed, and folding my too heavy limbs beneath me, I give him what he wants, totally unsure what it means for me. With my fingers gently kneading the tangle of his back, I wonder how long it'll be until I wear jeans again—if ever—and how long it will take me to forgive myself the experience of this man.

Shame becomes the color of his bedroom walls, his name in my mouth, the pile of all those many layers on the floor next to his bed. And all of the time it takes me to leave.

One book and a single earring. That is the extent of our entanglement upon ending. My mother tells me to let the earring go, ask him to put it in the mail, accept that he probably won't, and move on. But I've given him so much already, I'll be damned if he gets the earring, too.

On a Sunday afternoon before a matinee, I ring the buzzer at his apartment and wait. Patrick comes down two minutes later, trash bags in hand, and says he hasn't heard the bell—*Why didn't you ring it?*

I did, I say.

No, I would have heard it, he sputters back, anger erupting.

He goes back up for the earring and when he returns I hand him the book—*The Brief Wondrous Life of Oscar Wao*, only half read—and we both pause in the absence of a goodbye. Then I turn on my heel and walk away, tears rolling down my face.

I will quickly forget what restaurants we ate at or what it felt like to sit next to him in a theatre, but I will never forget what it feels like to walk away from him, west on 87th Street, towards the 1 train, towards other *maybes*.

CENTRAL PARK

Palma is the name of the cigar Noah buys from the bodega on 84th. He doesn't like the look of it. Doesn't like the green wrapper or trust the cheap packaging. But the man behind the counter has become impatient, weary of his blond, wavy hair, his earnest, youthful face. So Noah glances down at the cigar and gives in with a shrug. *Fine. Okay, this will do.*

Because it isn't really about the cigar.

It is the end of summer. I am only a few years out of college, still young enough at 25 to wear responsibility like an oversized coat I can cast off at a moment's notice. He is older, not by much, but enough. It is a setup. Emails are sent and we meet on a sunny afternoon outside of the Museum of Modern Art. We take one look at each other and laugh in that nervous way that signals relief. We spend hours wandering the museum's six floors before eating burritos on 54th Street. He is so handsome, with his tortoiseshell glasses, sleepy blue eyes, and beach-tousled hair. He has a smile that begins in the corner and spreads. It is easy, right from the start. We chat, without hesitation, about tennis and writing and our time in New York. *Everyone loves New York*, I say to him.

He smiles and says nothing, already knowing what it will take me years to learn, that almost no one loves it, but everyone lies about it.

It will end before it begins, with him leaving the city and returning home to the Blue Ridge Mountains of Virginia. Not long after, he will tour the world, playing guitar in a well-known band, and I will marvel from afar, quietly giddy at the twists and turns life has in store for us all. But long before he makes his living as touring musician, when he is just about to leave the city, we spend his last night in New York on a small, sloping hill set just off the path in Central Park. There, sitting cross-legged, his guitar to my right, I watch as he lights the cigar, the packaging so easily discarded, his blond curls casting a shadow across his face.

I feel like I'm seventeen, I say, with a slow smile, a soft laugh, a long, deep breath of smoke. *Palllmmmmma*. I like the sound of the name. Like how the *l* into the *m* feels in my mouth. My one act of teenage rebellion was smoking cigars with the boys from my graduating class on the soccer field of a local elementary school. Life was easy then. There was so much to look forward to, and so much to fear, too, but we didn't know that then. Our biggest worries were about which college we'd attend or if we'd miss that night's curfew.

Noah and I are too alike; there is affection, but not enough. I catch his thoughts in the middle, certain they're already finished. And so we bid farewell to one another—and he to New York—lying on our backs, our shoulders lightly touching, a single cigar passed between us, the night sky an expanse of stars barely visible beyond the city skyline.

ON HOME

"The female doesn't want a rich or a handsome man or even a poet, she wants a man who understands her eyes if she gets sad, and points to his chest and says: Here is your home country."
Nizar Qabbani

I put shallots in everything and call them scallions because I cannot remember their name. I'm a sucker for fresh flowers—mostly small, unwieldy ones straining skyward—*Ranunculus*, which means "little frog" in Latin. Sometimes I eat tortilla chips in the shower. Or under the bedcovers. Or barefoot in the kitchen before I've even poured my morning coffee—and I really like my morning coffee. On days when I'm feeling blue I'll get a latte just for the warmth between my hands.

Ask me to dance. On the subway platform, at the bar, in the living room. Not because I can, or you can, but because who cares? Because it doesn't matter if we're any good. Because you'd use any excuse just to place the palm of your hand on the small of my back. Because the last guy didn't.

Tell me I'm beautiful. Even if I already know you think I am, and you know that I know, tell me again, tell me anyway. Tell me once more than is reasonable or necessary.

And when I call you in hysterics, when I collapse into you undone by something you think small and ridiculous, just the moment before your impulse to fix everything kicks in, give me three words: *I hear you.*

I believe in love. In the mess of it, and the grace of it, and—frankly—in the mundanity of it. In crawling into bed night after night next to it. Because sometimes you just need a person to be quiet with, and sad next to.

HELL'S KITCHEN

Olivia lives in a fifth-floor walk-up on 51st and 9th. So much of my first two years at Juilliard is shaped by the fifteen blocks between college and her apartment. We have so much fun that first year. We spend Friday nights out with upperclassmen, at house parties and in bars, trading stories and sharing cabs. Occasionally we arrive home at five in the morning, and I collapse onto her couch before waking late the next morning to eat eggs and French fries at a diner two blocks up.

Sometimes I escape to her apartment midweek and spend the odd night on her couch. It is there we rehearse scenes and laugh about guys and complain about class-mates. Olivia is kind enough to suggest that perhaps falling in love with Will is a bad idea, but doesn't make me feel like a fool when I do exactly that.

There are eighteen of us in our year at college. Most days we spend twelve hours together, and that is just in class. Outside of class we argue and play and drink and see shows and marvel at the sheer luck of our existence in New York; though we are careful not to admit this aloud as we are still young enough to place a premium on "cool." We spend four years together in a single building fighting for our lives and our futures in a hundred different ways.

But everything feels uncertain and I want desperately to rush ahead, to see what comes next.

And then I become ill, and there is a sense that I am on the outside looking in. I sit in booths at cheap diners with classmates and feel increasingly isolated, the food on the table in front of me newly terrifying.

Olivia and I grow apart. I stop walking the fifteen blocks home with her after class.

My roommate is a young woman from Greece named Katerina. She studies the violin with Itzhak Perlman and tells stories about drinking wine and dancing in his foyer as she learns to make the instrument sing. Our friendship is not easy as we are incredibly different people, but within the confines of our tiny dorm room she is brutally honest, and so remarkably kind. She sees me for exactly who I am—a mess of disparate wants, a small universe in bloom. Sitting on our lofted beds one night she looks over at me and says, *So you thought you were going to come here and find people just like you. And you didn't. Well, now you're going to have to work a little bit harder.*

I don't find the women I adore in college, much as I want to. Instead I feel like I am losing friends as if through a sieve. But we are so young, and we know so little. And I am so sad, which is fair to no one. Instead I meet the women with whom I sit in dingy bars on 72nd Street discussing crummy men and frustrating teachers. The women with whom I gossip and laugh and do my best to pretend everything is fine. They are the women who sigh deeply and glance sideways at me, saying that at least I have my health, when it seems to me that it is the one thing I do not have.

★

I spend so much time after college wishing it all had gone differently. Wishing Will was my guy, wishing I was still an actor, wishing I was totally well, wanting badly to be able to spread my successes before me on a table and touch them, to prove my worth with something tangible. Instead I stop acting because I don't know how to be an actor while hating my body. I work in a restaurant at a job that I can't stand, and I return home in the evenings and sit at my small desk and write, but there is the constant question of what I am doing with my life, and I do not have an answer, not really.

A few years after college, Olivia calls and we end up one rainy afternoon sitting across from one another in a small café on the Upper West Side, my blue raincoat hanging from the back of my chair. We are eating pizza when Olivia pauses, smiles, and then gives me what no one else who knew me during that time could: an apology.

You were sick, and I laughed it off. You asked for help, and I said you didn't need it; I was wrong.

Surrounded by eighteen people for the four years of college, I spent most of the time standing on stages performing Chekhov and Shakespeare and Ibsen for audiences while feeling totally unseen in my own life. And then, years later, sitting in a café, Olivia says to me: *I did see you.*

When people say they cannot change, I think of Olivia. Because several years after college, we meet as changed women, more generous, more open, more willing to admit fault. Still in the middle of things, but with a little more life behind us, we pick up our friendship not where we left off, but on new ground, with forgiveness and kindness for who we were during those four years of college, and gratitude for the women we are becoming.

THE METROPOLITAN MUSEUM OF ART

I walk around the MET as things with a particular guy are unraveling. I am 26 years old, maybe 27, and, surrounded by such immense history and immeasurable beauty, I have but one thought: *There is a great, gaping hole in the middle of my chest.* I barely see any of the artwork.

How does one get over heartache? This question plagues me. I think about it on the subway and in the shower. I think about it as I lead people to numbered tables and collect their coats. I think about it as I hand young couples menus and wish them a very lovely dinner, sensing an invisible distance between us. I think about it as I spoon leftover Thai food from my small refrigerator at one in the morning and as I listen to Elliott Smith on the train home.

"I'm damaged bad at best," he sings in "Say Yes."[2] I am in debt to Elliott Smith for those five small and true words. I think about them as I meet men for the first

---

[2] Elliott Smith, "Say Yes" on *Either/Or* (Kill Rock Stars, 1997). Words and Music by Elliott Smith. Copyright © 1997 by Universal Music—Careers and Spent Bullets Music. All Rights Administered by Universal Music—Careers. International Copyright Secured. All Rights Reserved. Reprinted by Permission of Hal Leonard LLC.

time. First dates in which we sit at bars and sip wine and I wonder just how quickly they will see my sadness.

There are three years of my life I cannot remember. It is an uncomfortable truth and not easily explained. It happened so quietly, the moment I slipped from my life, that I cannot actually say when it occurred. I can only look back and guess. Was it on a long subway ride or a quiet morning? Was it in the middle of a crowded room, alone in a city that felt perpetually beyond reach?

I wear sadness differently now than I did at eighteen or 25 or any of the years between. I'm more comfortable with my own brokenness—more at ease with the notion that it's the well from which I draw empathy and kindness and humor. It is so telling of what it is to be human and alive in this world. But occasionally it is more immediate, closer to the surface. And I'm okay with that. It's an altogether not-so-bad feeling, sadness. Rather, it's the frustration, the sense of failure, the fear that I'll never be enough that I find altogether less than pleasurable— the mathematics of too much somehow adding up to not enough—too emotional, too honest, too demanding, too picky, too much of too many things. But altogether, not enough. Somehow, *still*, not enough. I'm damaged bad at best.

My mother says something that I can't stop thinking about. With great love she says, *You're afraid that everyone will figure out you're a fraud. You're afraid that everyone with something kind to say will figure out you're not worthy of their belief in you. And that's on you.* She says it and shame rises unbidden, coloring my cheeks because I know it is true.

On first dates I think: please don't let this man tell me I'm beautiful. Please don't let him reach for my knee. Please, please don't let his hand touch my hand because "palm to palm is holy palmers' kiss" and—holy hell—it really is the best part. Because should those things happen, he might like me. And as soon as he likes me, he'll stumble upon that thing that makes me unlovable. That one thing that I can't name and can't see and can't place, but am so sure is there. And as soon as he does, he'll leave.

I've never once said anything honest and true to a man I've cared for. I lost years of my life to loving Will and the closest I got to telling him was with seven words: *I think you're a pretty fine guy.* Seven words when I only needed three. And a bit of courage.

But I am not a courageous person.

I don't know how we get over heartache, only that we do. The movement of each man from a maybe to a no has cut a path wide and deep through my core, adding something to that wellspring of sadness. But the best and worst and truest and saddest thing that no one ever talks about is this: there's always someone else. The heart goes in search of love, always. Even—and most especially—when we don't want it to. And thus the war is a silent one, fought on the home front, between a heart that propels us forward and a body that doesn't think it'll survive another go.

But I hold fast to another hope: that there will be a person who will see the sadness right away and will know it's not so bad. That there will be a man who will touch my knee and grab my hand, who will trace the outline of my curves and connect the dots of my moles and will come up for air and say, *I can't find it. That thing you're convinced that'll make me run—I can't find it.* The truth is, we are all damaged bad at best, and we are all still worthy.

INFINITIES

A n infinity.

This is the timeline of events:

At nineteen I stand in front of a mirror and convince myself I am fat. It takes me five minutes to rewire a small bit of the brain that perceives weight and shape. Five minutes. An infinity.

At twenty I starve myself for two months. Ten weeks actually. Such an insignificant amount of time. And yet, another infinity.

For the next three years I binge. My body balloons, and every bit of who I am as a person shrinks in direct proportion. For three years an illness hijacks my every thought and every action, and it feels like I am drowning in plain sight. An infinity.

Five years trudging towards recovery. Slowly breath returns and inch by inch ground is gained. Things get better. And I get better. But there is always more to go: "And miles to go before I sleep."[3]

I have a conversation with one of my dearest friends, Alice, one gray afternoon when I am just beginning to

---

[3] Robert Frost, "Stopping by Woods on a Snowy Evening" in *The Poetry of Robert Frost*, ed. Edward Connery Lathem (New York: Henry Holt and Company, 1969; poem 1923).

get better. Alice and I met when I was 23, working at a restaurant on 54th and 3rd. She was older than me by a month and nearly a full foot shorter. She was perky and enthusiastic and from Florida, and I disliked her immediately. We went to work each day wearing cheap black suits, our hair pulled tight into buns, and we would wipe down tables and transfer bar tabs as we rubbed elbows with New York's moneyed elite, not really having enough to pay our bills. The economy had just collapsed and everyone was on edge. A career in the arts—which is what we were after—felt like a fool's errand. Slowly I realized her enthusiasm was a savvy and subversive trick to mask her biting wit and unparalleled intelligence. And, as soon as I realized that, I was half in love with her.

We sit across from one another, and I tell her I am blue and low and bruised, and she looks me right in the eye and says, *Meg, we all have those moments. We all live through stretches of time in which we think we're not doing so well.* And as I listen to her I suddenly feel a distance between us that is unbridgeable. I am aware that we are using similar words to describe two very different experiences. *That's not what this is,* I want to say. *We're not talking about the same thing.* But instead I sip my coffee and smile and nod because, much as we don't always want them to be, some battles are private ones.

When I am deep in the throes of the eating disorder people often ask what brings on a binge. And at that time I do not know—cannot say—which is a particular, crippling sort of frustration. I know that it is mostly a feeling, but I cannot say what that feeling is. The truth is I am mistaking many feelings for one. And so the process of getting better is the act of untangling each, holding them up to the light one by one and giving them a name: anxiety, which is different to fear, which is different to sadness, which is different to frustration, which is different to anger. And depression, which is different to just a usual stretch of time in which one isn't doing so well.

★

Sometimes, while walking home, or standing on the subway, or sitting across from a girlfriend sipping coffee, I am still struck by how physical a feeling can be, and I'll think: *Existing in this physical form, in this particular moment, is nearly unbearable*. I used to think, *I hate my body*. But as it turns out, "I hate my body" was reductive. My thinking brain was attempting to make something incredibly complicated and nuanced easily understood. But it was wrong: I didn't hate my body, I hated the experience of inhabiting my body, which is an altogether different thing. But because I didn't understand that, or didn't have words for it, I said again and again, *I hate my body, I hate my body, I hate my body*. I said it so many times that it became true.

The very best thing that came from grappling with an eating disorder is the ability to sit with uncomfortable feelings, to study them, to bring them out into the light.

Just the other day I was walking east on 49th Street and thought, *I'm not doing so well. I'm having a rough time.* And quick on the heels of that thought came another: *This must be the not-so-good that everyone always told me about. I'm right now, at this very moment, going through a totally normal rough patch.* And heaven was that thought—heaven was that notion of a shallower, more bearable, not so overwhelming not-so-good.

This is a new infinity that will dwarf those that came before.

WILLIAMSBURG

You meet a person and immediately go from being strangers to something else, his hand reaching for your thigh under the table. And maybe you meet again and something is shared—a late night cab in the rain from the south of Brooklyn to the east.

And then one person, or both—but rarely both—decides they no longer want to share that something else. And poof. You are strangers again. Somehow stranger than before. And you live in this city for months or years and lead these parallel lives and then one day, when you least expect it, you look up to find you're staring at this man.

You don't yet know it's him. You catch him out of the corner of your eye and think little of it. But for some reason you feel the need to look again. And awareness creeps around the back of your neck. Dark brown hair, rolled jeans, sneakers, the start of a beard. Then you see the chain around his neck and that's all it takes—a small silver strand—and suddenly you can't breathe. Your hand goes to the cut just below your left breastbone that has taken too long to heal.

★

George kissed me ferociously on the subway train that first night, pausing only to come up for air. We sat on the L for twenty minutes, waiting for it to move east along its 14th Street route, and as we sat there he took my hand in his and kissed my neck moving up and over towards my mouth. We'd met earlier in the evening and he had kissed both my cheeks in greeting. *As is the custom where I'm from*, he'd explained, his British accent low and rich and wildly disorienting in all the best ways. We'd then sat on opposite sides of a booth in the Soho House on the edge of the Meatpacking District. As I approached the table that night I felt a small pang of disappointment that he wasn't as handsome as I'd hoped, but then he got up and came to sit next to me, and when his hand reached for my thigh it was both a surprise and a small revolution, my stomach turning circles over itself. I was nuts about him from that moment forward.

Until of course, so suddenly after, so without warning, he decided he did not want to know me anymore.

And now here he is, five feet away, at an outdoor bar on the side of Williamsburg where I know he doesn't live. I pretend not to recognize him and wonder if he's seen me. Perhaps not —my hat is large and my sunglasses dark.

I am with a group of friends and so I turn to the boy next to me with his floppy hair and sleepy eyes and ask him to look at me for just, like, ten minutes, as if I'm the most beautiful girl in the world. And I wrap my rapidly burning shoulders in his oversized button-down shirt because I suddenly feel so very exposed, naked to more than the late July sun. And for a moment he gives me that loopy, lazy grin that comes so naturally to politicians and movie stars and boys who only think they've been in love. But then he turns back to the group too quickly, and I am left to my own experience, a very private one, in this very public place.

George is with someone. And she is so obviously cooler than me. Lithe and pretty and funky in that way I've always envied in other women. She's wearing cutoffs and mirrored sunglasses, and is all long limbs and short hair. I sit there, still as I can, wondering if he will say hello, both terrified that he will and terrified that he won't.

The last time I saw him I'd arrived at his apartment in the pouring rain. He'd answered the door naked and taken me to bed quickly. As soon as he finished I placed my hand on his leg and he threw it off mumbling something about not liking to sleep all tangled limbs—*not even with the girl he'd loved for many years*. And I'd lain there, still as I could, my eyes wide, staring at the ceiling above. His hand found mine in the dark and squeezed: once, twice, three times, a pause between each, waiting for my response. Instead I'd slipped my hand out of his and turned on my side, quiet tears making their way to the pillow below. I wondered in that moment, my face wet and hot, if he'd find my mascara on his sheets the next day, and if when he saw it, he'd know what it meant. The next morning he kicked me out of bed just ten minutes before he had to be up for a phone call, and I took the train from Williamsburg to Carroll Gardens, knowing I should have left the night before, sure I shouldn't have gone over at all.

Sitting at the bar, my mind wanders to the man I began dating just after George. My best girlfriend and I had escaped into a small West Village restaurant, and David had been at the other end of a long, communal table, part of a group of six guys. He paused on his way out, chatted breezily, called me charming, and then invited me to dinner—the invitation more a demand than anything else. I'd been done in by his supreme confidence, his absolute nerve. I'd given him my best hair-flip and half-smile and said, *Yes, dinner.* It was on our second date that he told me not to fall in love with him, and I'd laughed, assuring him I had no intention of letting that happen. And I meant it.

In the time since, he has said again and again how shy he is, and I know this to be a lie, but I play along. *Why, then, did you approach me that first night?* I ask coyly. And he answers with one word, *Irresistible.* And somehow, in his less than perfect English, with his lilting Brazilian accent, that one word is enough. It is a little truthful, and a little not—and I know this—but it is true enough that I smile in a way that is as close to just-for-him as I can manage and tuck my head beneath his chin.

Whatever it is the two of us have been building is a flimsy thing—a we're-never-going-to-love-each-other-but-isn't-this-nice sort of thing. Already I know we are on borrowed time—that it's only lasted as long as it has because we met at a time when loneliness flitted at the edge of every image, threatening and ever-present.

But already I've learned so much from this man who doesn't love me, this man with no intention of ever loving me, this man who doesn't actually think love exists. This man who pays for dinner and refuses to smoke in my presence. Who offers to call the airline for me and reminds me to wish my mother a happy Mother's Day. This man who is so not the right guy, but who cares for me as he knows how and holds me close when he can. This man I will meet one lazy Saturday afternoon years from now, who will buy me a drink and say hello and kiss me softly and ask how I am and actually want to know. This man who will never pretend not to know me.

George doesn't say hello—this now-stranger with his half-beard, vintage sunglasses, and *Wall Street Journal* byline. He barely looks at me, but he knows I am there. I finger the cut on my chest that I woke to after that first night, thinking probably it was the chain around his neck that dug into me, as his body pressed in hard on mine in the middle of the night. We'd both slept so fitfully. And he'd pushed his penis into me in the early morning hours, while we were both still half asleep. It had been lovely and good, but hours later when he said, off-handedly, that he hadn't worn a condom, it was I who went to the drugstore, alone, and I who pulled out my wallet to pay for that small white pill, thankful for the choice, but still sick with the shame of it.

I turn back to my friend with his lazy smile, rest my head on his shoulder and sip the wine in front of me. I laugh when I'm meant to and pretend that I'm fine. Because I am, mostly. The cut on my chest, still red, has long since stopped hurting. Eventually everything else will too.

WEST 10TH STREET

You've *lost weight*, David says, his hands tracing the underside of my breasts, as we lie in bed.

Maybe, I reply, my lips quickly finding his mouth in an effort to redirect.

Before long he asks again, *Have you been going to the gym a lot?*

Nope. Not any more than before.

It is late when I stand to dress, the apartment mostly dark, a single lamp in the corner. As I pull my blouse over my head, I can feel him watching, his eyes studying my curves, *No, Meg, you've lost a lot of weight. Seriously.*

I don't talk about my weight, and I mostly expect that no one else will either.

I don't know, David. Maybe, I say, a little exasperated, as I lean over his coffee table looking for my shoes.

Yeah, because, like, you were a little chubby before, no?

And there it is. The word "chubby" hangs in the air for a moment as I catch my tongue between my teeth. I pause with one hand on the floor, the other on his side table, only one shoe on. I turn slowly to face him, my eyebrows raised, my eyes wide.

You can't say that, David. You can't say that to a girl. Ever.

It takes him a moment to catch up. Honest to God, the man has to sort through what has just been said in order to figure out where he's gone wrong. We remain frozen in position, breaths held, wondering who will speak next.

But, but I'm saying—well, I'm saying you're not anymore, he stammers. *It's better now. I'm saying it's better now*, his trademark cool reduced to a low-level panic.

When David and I go on dates there always comes a moment—towards the beginning of the date, but not too early in—when he sort of cocks his head, looks at me sideways and says, *You know, you really are quite beautiful*—as though he hasn't realized until right then. It always makes me laugh because it is as though he has no memory for what I look like, which has a way of making beauty—that elusive and disastrous and terribly important thing that is beauty—secondary to everything else. He says it not as a compliment, or as a means to an end, just as an observation.

But now, in his dimly lit apartment, with my bag in hand and only one shoe on, I take a breath, pull my hair behind me, fish my other shoe out from under the bed, and look right at him: *David, you cannot call a girl chubby. Past tense or not, you just can't.*

Oh, well, you know, my English isn't perfect, he demurs.

Which is true, it really isn't. But it's good enough, and he is a decidedly smart man.

The next morning over breakfast with my friend Mary, I tell her the story. And she smiles at me and with her PhD brain says, *You know, Meg, there could be a cultural gap there. He wasn't making a value judgment on chubby or not chubby. He only said that one was better than the other after you'd sufficiently sucked all of the air from the room.*

Oh God. She is right, of course. I laugh as soon as she says it, and find I can't stop. There, in the brightly lit restaurant in Carroll Gardens, over eggs and sausage and candied pecans, I laugh because David and I don't love one another, not really. And I laugh because once upon a time I was chubby and now I'm not, and neither matters. I laugh because beauty is an illusion and a ridiculous one at that. I laugh because life keeps moving forward and, against all odds, I'm okay.

ON HOME, II

I have this recurring fantasy. It involves wooden floors and the song "Isn't She Lovely." You're wearing boxer briefs, and I'm in one of your oversized t-shirts, a relic of youth and college and years long since passed. We both have on clean white ankle socks. You know how to dance, I do not. We push the furniture to the edge of the room, and you sing—badly—spinning me with your arm raised above our heads, our socks turning circles on the floor, night giving way to morning.

Don't take me to the opera. Don't take me to the Rainbow Room. Don't make it a carriage ride through Central Park or a weekend getaway. I'm not even sure I need you to get down on one knee. But sit next to me on the doorstep, on the front stoop, and with your hand cupping my neck promise me quiet Sunday mornings with coffee and the paper and unfinished crossword puzzles. Promise me the arm that reaches out when I step off the curb a moment too soon. An extra set of hands to pull at my zipper or put the groceries away. Flowers for no reason at all. The coffee brewed before I wake. Passed arts sections and shared looks and your hand on my knee for as long as we both shall live. Dancing in the kitchen, bare feet and no music except for that song wetting your lips.

TRIBECA

I am 27 the first time I see Eric and am immediately struck by the clarity of his image. It is as though everything else has been ever so slightly out of focus and I hadn't realized until the moment this man—this very handsome man with his sharp angles and neatly trimmed hair—first stands in front of me. I am still working at the restaurant and he is speaking to the maître d' when he glances over. I feel caught, exposed. He makes a joke, and I give a barely audible laugh. He is so handsome, and I am so quiet; handsome men always make me quiet.

It is my girlfriend, Alice, who asks, after I have gone, if he wants my number. He says yes and sends a lovely message, and we make a plan to meet.

And then he stands me up. On our first date—a late night drink. I sit there for 30 minutes and take two sips of wine before collecting my things to go. The bartender doesn't ask me to pay and I don't offer. I call Alice, and we decide he has a wife or a girlfriend and has come to his senses.

I wake the next morning to a message. *I'm an idiot*, it says. *I slept through my alarm.* When I tell my girlfriends they say to forget him, that it's not a good excuse. Instead I reply, *Glad to know you're just an idiot, and not an asshole.*

And so we try again. A second first date. I make him come a little further east, and I wear flats, with my hair a messy knot atop my head. When I order my first glass of wine I have to angle my body away from him because my hand is shaking so badly from nerves that I can't read the small print on the menu.

The date is fine. Simple and fine. No fireworks, just a quiet sort of unfolding. In fact, my strongest impression is of how warm the night is. It is early July and my legs stick to the barstool beneath me. When I walk away from him I think, *If that's all this is, a fine first date, that's okay.*

But because I am a sucker for a good story, and the way in which we met felt like exactly that—chance encounter, locked eyes, missed first date—we try again two weeks later, and I gloss over the bad. Like how on that oppressively hot night in July he didn't offer to take my heavy bag as we walked away from the bar. Or how on our second date he complains about the table instead of simply asking the waiter to move us. How his body never inches towards me—how his hand never brushes against mine.

He has a dinner party at his home a few months after we begin dating. Eric lives in a large apartment in Tribeca on the 39th floor of a high-rise with a view that stretches for miles in all directions—the apartment feels more of the sky than of the earth. The view of the new World Trade Center is immediate and remarkable. He tells me the woman who lived there before him watched as the second plane hit the tower, and moved out the month after. His furniture is sparse and clean, and the walls are unadorned. The dining room table is nearly perfect—a smooth green, milky glass, with a single, barely noticeable scratch marring one side. *Someone dragged a pot across it*, he says when he catches me looking at it. I can hear the annoyance in his voice.

Eric sits at the head of the table, and I find myself on the other end, seated next to a friend of a friend who is new to New York. When she asks how we met, Eric glosses over the fact that I was working at a restaurant, and I realize he is embarrassed by this. That I am unimpressive to him in this way. I sip my wine slowly, but by the end of the night there are twelve empty bottles piled in the bin next to the kitchen counter. Twelve bottles for ten people, and I am only on my second glass—it is an uncomfortable math. I feel so sober as I sit there, staring at that spot on the table, smiling and laughing at this man's bad jokes and feeling like I am on the outside looking in.

Towards the end of the night there are only four of us. Eric and his best friend and his best friend's girl-friend, a woman whom I know he dislikes because he has detailed at length, on more than one occasion, how needy and demanding she is. And he is right. I can see immediately that his description of her is accurate, but I also see that she is achingly insecure—unwilling to play games with the rest of us for fear of looking foolish.

She is beautiful, with thick dark hair, long legs, and deeply freckled shoulders. But as soon as it is just the four of us she begins to make fun of the woman I'd sat next to during dinner. Her hair, her body, how unremarkable-looking she found her. Her boyfriend sits there quietly, but Eric joins in. *Ah, well, she's 32—I'd never date a 32-year-old*, he says. I wonder in that moment what difference it makes to a 35-year-old-man. Eric then turns his body towards this woman—Katie, I think her name is—and when Katie, with her long dark hair and freckled shoulders tells a joke he laughs in a way that he has never before laughed for me. I catch my breath and think, *Oh, well, there's that.*

I nearly leave in that moment. Nearly grab my jacket and bag and quietly slip out the front door. Instead I go to the bathroom, study my reflection, listen as they whisper, not able to hear what is being said, knowing I'm not meant to, their muted voices punctuated by someone's laughter.

When the night ends, Eric asks me to stay. And so we climb into bed, side by side. I wear one of his t-shirts and he turns away as I pull it over my head. He sleeps, I do not. For the second time that night, I hide in the bathroom, this time shivering, trying to sort quickly through my own tangle of emotions. The next morning, riding the train to work, I quietly weep. I can feel the woman across from me watching; I let her.

★

It was on our third date, having dinner at the Wythe in Brooklyn, that Eric and I spoke of regrets.

I said I mostly only regretted small things—frozen moments. That time last January when a man squeezed my hand and I didn't squeeze his back. Or how when I was seven I didn't crawl into my grandmother's lap, and how sad that made her. How there wasn't time enough to go again because life ends at different times for different people. And how at the age of twenty, blue in way that knew no words, I couldn't say just one word—*yes*—when asked if I needed help.

Sitting at a small table, wine between us and not enough light, he said he would have regretted not saying hello, and I believed him.

But sitting on the floor of his bathroom in the middle of the night, and riding the train the next morning, I regret that he did. And I regret everything that followed.

JOHN F. KENNEDY INTERNATIONAL AIRPORT

I bound down the narrow staircase, a tangle of nerves and excitement and too many carry-ons. My small suitcase twists uncomfortably behind me as I navigate bags and anxiety and the sort of scarf that doubles as a blanket. I am breathless and a little unkempt but, dressed in my darkest coat and a wide-brimmed hat, I feel utterly beautiful.

I reach the landing, straighten up, take a breath, and am surprised to find him standing just on the other side of the door. He is standing so very still, his dark curls still wet against his head, his button-down so neatly pressed.

I had expected Eric to be in the car or waiting on the sidewalk. And something about the immediacy of his presence unnerves me. But I grin, untangle my bags, and wait for his response.

He doesn't move. Doesn't smile or tilt his head or even register that he has seen me through the glass. I must look at him strangely in this moment because he finally glances down and then pushes open the front door.

My chest tightens immediately. My thoughts snagging on this moment, pulling me back. I am aware as I stand there staring at him through the glass that I now know something I can't un-know, although I'm still totally unsure as to what that thing is.

I shrug it off, choose not to think about it. After all, we are going to Paris. Paris! The city with a name so light that to say it feels like little more than an exhalation—warm breath on a cold window, a little foggy, but mostly magic. Paris must not be overthought.

We hug, he kisses my cheek, takes my bag. *You sure you still want to do this?* I ask, laughing nervously. *It's much easier to back out now than at the airport.*

Of course, he says without smiling, turning away from me towards the car, mentioning traffic in the tunnel.

Once situated in the cab, my large open-mouthed purse resting on the floor between us, my passport visible, he asks to see it.

He looks at it for so long. Too long. So long I feel the need to say, *It's nearly ten years old—don't I look different?* Smiling as women do when they know they are still young, but not so young as they once were.

You can't travel on this, he says finally, without looking up at me.

What? I ask. *What are you talking about?*

It has to be valid three months after your date of return, and this is not.

Wait, really? I ask, a nervous laugh breaking from my mouth.

Yes.

Silence.

He lifts his head, and I see that a hollow sort of look has clouded his eyes—not quite anger, something else. My mind again snags on that first moment I saw him through the door.

We call the airline, or rather, he calls at my urging. They don't think it will be a problem; the trip is only four days. I take a breath, *It's okay. See? It's okay.*

It's not going to be okay, he responds, staring straight ahead, his three passports tucked safely in his carry-on.

Well, at least this will make for a good story, I say, turning to look at him, attempting to smile. *If it works out*, he says, not meeting my eyes.

I spend much of the remaining ride staring out the window as he asks the driver about the traffic and alternative routes. When he finally reaches his arm out, an attempt to comfort, I am struck by how touch can be a distancing thing.

I read something once in a memoir by Anna Quindlen about how young couples rarely think about how their partner will react when racing to the hospital with a sick child in the backseat.[4] I think about that passage on the way to the airport because this is not even close—this is an invalid passport, an honest mistake—and he can barely look at me.

---

[4] Anna Quindlen, *Lots of Candles, Plenty of Cake: A Memoir*. (New York: Random House, 2012), p. 17

When we get to the airport, the ticket agent goes through all the steps, asks all the right questions, looks so very sorry for me when she tells me I cannot go. Eric gives me a hundred dollar bill for the cab ride home, and I walk away, my packed bag trailing behind me.

He goes to Paris. And I do not.

In the weeks leading up to the trip, whenever I'd tell someone I was going away for the weekend the first question was always *Where?* And I sort of catch my breath, tilt my head, and whisper, *Paris.*

With your boyfriend? Was always, without fail, the follow-up.

No.

With some girlfriends?

No.

And then would come the inevitable pause, the small quizzical smile, the subtle squint of the eyes. And I'd say, *A guy—a friend. We're just friends.*

And everyone would sort of chuckle. Because they sensed my hesitation, my own obvious confusion.

We'll see, they'd say.

Eric and I had broken up twice already. We were not right together. But we had gone to dinner just before Christmas, and he'd been the first person to message when the clock struck twelve at the start of the New Year. And on a whim he had invited me to Paris, and who was I to say no? And some small part of me wondered if it might yet work, and what we might yet be.

So many questions. All of the answers in France.

Except when you don't go. Except when the ticket agent smiles so very apologetically after telling you that your passport, while still valid, is not valid to travel on, and then nods to the next guest, but the man standing next to you looks at her and says, *Well, I'm still going.* And then turns to you, *You get that I still have to go, right?* And well, no, actually, you don't. Because he's not going for business, and there is nothing there for him but the trip the two of you had planned together. So, suddenly, all those questions are answered at a ticket counter at an airport in Queens.

I go looking for that paragraph—the one about the sick child in the backseat. On the Saturday morning, just two days after I am meant to go to Paris with Eric, I pull it off the bookshelf.

It is so underwhelming on the page, sandwiched between other examples of how people mostly don't choose their partner while considering worst-case scenarios: "the two of you at 40 driving a kid to the emergency room with blood on the backseat." It is less than a sentence, but how large it seemed in my memory says more about me than anything has in quite some time.

And I suddenly know. I suddenly know Eric is not the man I'd want *driving a kid to the emergency room.* Which means he sure as hell is not the man I want holding my hand when bad news comes, as it surely will. So thank God he will not be the man standing beside me when I see for the first time the Seine or the Pont Neuf or the Eiffel Tower glittering in the distance.

No phone calls were made. No attempts to shuffle or reroute. He didn't even walk the hundred feet to put me in a cab home. All of which I might have been able to forgive. But that he didn't smile when I first came down the stairs, that he had no response at all, I can't forgive that.

★

I was wrong about him. Which is a truth that is hard to sit with. He was average. He lived in a perpetual state of preparation for the next Worst Thing—holding everything and everyone at arm's length, thinking he could outsmart sadness, as though it had anything to do with that, as though he weren't missing out on life all the while.

I think back now to our first meeting and how he seemed in sharp focus. The clarity didn't come so much from how handsome he was, as from how very present he seemed, like he was right there at the front of himself. And I was awed by this because I hardly ever am. But now I know it's tremendously easy to live at the front of yourself if that's all there is.

I was so lonely when we dated. I had just started a new job and was working more typical hours, and so I thought it was an evening sort of loneliness. I thought it was a going-home-to-an-empty-apartment-at-the-age-of-27 sort of loneliness. A *still?* sort of loneliness. But then we stopped dating. And I wasn't so lonely anymore.

Turns out it was a this-isn't-the-right-guy-and-you-know-it-but-won't-admit-it sort of loneliness. Which is a more brutal variety because it has everything to do with you. Everything to do with that small tug of the gut that says, *Move on, you know better.* But it's hard to be 27 with the thought that you've never done it right before and maybe you're doing it all wrong—and what the hell does the gut know anyway?

Being with Eric wasn't all bad of course. It would be easy to say that it was, but time passed quickly when we were together, and we never ran out of things to say. On occasion, he would even lean back in his chair and look at me like he could sit there forever, and I am a woman who wants few things more than to be looked at like that, often.

But while few things are so exciting as slowly unfolding in front of someone you adore, trying to do so in front of a person you're just not that keen on is confusing and unsettling and leaves you months later in a cab on the way to the airport barely breathing because you all of a sudden cannot stand this person. And that's not really fair to him because he's not all bad, he's just not right.

He had no interest in seeing me naked. Which is an interesting problem to confront as a woman. There is a small list of men to whom I owe a great debt. Men who adored my body when I loathed it most. Men who revealed my beauty in the way their upper teeth caught their lower lips as I undressed. Men whose gazes pulled me across a very large, very deep chasm—one that separated understanding beauty from inhabiting it. Before Eric I knew what it was to be ashamed of my feminine form, but I didn't know what it was to feel that shame while standing naked in front of a man. I remember asking him that night of the dinner party if he really liked me. And he breathed out a long sigh, placed his head down next to mine, and without looking at me, said: *Of course, I do. I adore you*, that thinly veiled annoyance in his voice.

Eric's words never lined up with his actions, and reconciling those two things was a lonely road I traveled alone.

He had lost his mother too young. And that informed everything about him. My heart broke for him and the truth of that loss. But it had turned some part of him cruel, and he made himself a victim of the capriciousness of That Which We Cannot Control. Which is to say, both life and death. And you cannot get close to, or be intimate with, or fall in love with a person who is so mired in their own shit that they'll do anything they can to pretend there's not a stink about it. You can only wish them well and walk away.

It turns out that so much of growing up is about walking away from That Which is Not Right in pursuit of something better.

BRYANT PARK

"The power of a glance has been so much abused in love stories, that it has come to be disbelieved. Few people dare now to say that two beings have fallen in love because they looked at each other. Yet it is in this way that love begins, and in this way only."

Victor Hugo, *Les Miserables*

I feel Jack before I see him. That first day I look up, and there he is, standing in the lobby, all tan-skinned and tall and unnerving, his lips parted ever so slightly. He has this goofy look on his face—one of mild surprise, like he's been caught mid-thought. I don't believe in love at first sight, I really don't, but I sure as hell believe in whatever I felt that first time I saw him: a tidal wave of *Oh shit*.

I begin the job at the start of September, but Jack and I don't speak until November. No one introduces us and neither of us is courageous enough to thrust out a hand and say hello. Once, though, in those first few weeks, as I am collecting glasses and water pitchers, I look up to find his eyes on me. He is standing at his desk, twenty paces away, chatting into the phone, the whole of his body turned towards me. I hold his gaze for as long as I can, my eyes finding the floor only after my cheeks flush red. Our only exchange in those first two months is when, in a moment of unexpected bravery, I manage to ask him where he is going in response to the overnight bag in his hand. Jack answers with a grin and a word—*California*—his body already out the door. Westward. He feels like his own sort of frontier.

I was nothing if not afraid. It feels important to say that now, by way of explanation. Or apology.

By November the two of us pause to chat in the kitchen. We talk about small things: where we live and where we are from. Information is parsed slowly and tentatively. He asks for my help one morning, and late in the afternoon comes to my desk, a coffee mug in hand, just to chat and say thank you. He stands there, sipping his coffee slowly, one hand pushed deep into the pocket of his slacks, and I am out of my depth, confused by his kindness, unsure of his interest. Occasionally, when the office is empty and we've both stayed late, I'll stop in front of his desk—*See you tomorrow*—and Jack will nod several times, pursing his lips. We mostly don't smile easily around one another.

I like to sneak glances at him when I can. And occasionally, when I'm lucky, he does the same. Once, I call out to him as he passes—saying something silly, nothing really—and Jack looks over his shoulder and, without breaking his stride, gives me this wide, loose grin, unguarded and happy. And it strikes me that his response is so disproportionate to what I have said, but so perfectly apt for what is happening in the meaty and wordless territory where two people meet. It feels like standing in the sun on the first day of spring after a very long winter. *I did that*, I think as he walks away. *That smile—I did that.* Twenty-eight years and I'd never had that thought before.

There is a holiday party at the start of December. I don't know too many people and so pause near the entrance, tilting back on my heels, taking in the space. I begin chatting with the men behind the bar. *Something strong*, I request. Barely looking at me, his hands deftly organizing the bottles, one of the guys asks, *Vodka-based? Gin? Whiskey?*

Whiskey.

An Old-fashioned? A Manhattan?

Just whiskey. Neat. Drinking straight whiskey is my very best party trick and the most effective way I know to flirt.

The bartender pauses, his hand now hovering, and turns to take me in. I hold his gaze, coolly, and then I grin in that way that sees my teeth grip tightly to the side of my lower lip. He smiles at me, shaking his head in that barely perceptible way, a soft laugh escaping from his lips. *I'm not supposed to do this, but I'm going to pour from this bottle, and keep it here*, he says, pointing to a spot just off to the side, *for when you want some more.*

Jack approaches the bar, standing on the other side of the corner, by himself, and orders a beer. I watch as the gold liquid fills his glass. We both stand there awkwardly, holding our breath. I start to say something, he glances at me, and then someone pulls him away. *Almost*.

Eric once explained to me that men approach the bar when the woman they want to talk to is standing there. Years later a friend will tell me that while studying abroad he'd toss his glass of water out the open window just to have a reason to go into the kitchen and flirt with his housemate.

My eyes go in search of Jack not long after and find him across the room, wearing a dark blue blazer and looking handsome as few men have any right to, his eyes already on me. I glance behind me, sure he is looking at someone else. I cannot understand how someone so handsome—with his Kennedy hair, light eyes, and movie-star good looks—might find me attractive. But his gaze isn't calculated or aware; it isn't a means to an end. He simply is a man who looks because he cannot not look. And with his eyes on me and my knees weak, I feel like enough. Scared as I am, around Jack I always feel like enough.

Jack pauses before he leaves that night, his charcoal overcoat—the one he wears on special occasions—already on. *Hello and goodbye*, he says. I grab his arm above the elbow, my fingers tentative but firm, the whiskey warm in my stomach. *Don't go. Have another drink*, I say. And there we stand, frozen in position, me with my hand above his elbow, him with his coat on, saying a little, but not enough—afraid of what those around us might see or say, afraid of what we both already know but can't yet admit. *Almost*.

I leave the party not long after. Sat on a crowded subway, I close my eyes and feel the motion of the train. It is in a tunnel somewhere between Manhattan and Brooklyn that I realize he had said to me, *You look really beautiful tonight*. But in the moment, I hadn't heard him.

The next day at work he takes the long loop around my desk, tapping a soda can between his hands, looking at me without actually turning his head, as though it's somehow less obvious. *Just needed to stretch my legs*, he says, lying. God I am nuts about him. Him and his goofy grin and perfect teeth and low voice. The way he musses his hair and swings between total confidence and a sort of panic so specific to grown men. And how his broad hands always seem like they have a bit of dirt beneath the fingernails.

It is in January that I ruin it. He's just returned from Christmas break and I am newly nervous in front of him—something about too much time passing and not enough courage and how damn tan vacation has made him. Looking at Jack is like looking at the sun—good and overwhelming and a little bit blinding. I had just gotten up from my desk to pass a message on to someone, and he is there when I return. He says hello and wishes me a happy New Year, his voice buoyant and light—hopeful, even. He looks so handsome standing there, so at ease. And as I sit down I take one look at him and cock my head to the side as though I cannot understand why he is speaking to me. It is self-preservation of the highest order and it is at his expense. Because to reveal anything would be to reveal everything and I am afraid.

"We are all fools in love," Jane Austen wrote in *Pride and Prejudice*. I always misunderstood that line until this man. I thought it was a description of mankind—foolish and often in love. I didn't understand that what she meant was that love makes fools of otherwise reasonable people.

It is a terrible mistake, of course—quick and imperceptible to anyone passing by, but with devastating consequences. Later, I'll come back to this moment and wish I could undo it. In fact, if I could undo any one thing from the whole terrible mess of this year, it would be this moment on Monday morning, six days into the new year, when I barely meet Jack's eyes and mumble, *Yeah, fine, happy New Year*, shuffling the papers in front of me, pretending he doesn't matter.

People tell you that you can't ruin love. That such a small thing can't undo such a big thing. But when that thing is true and good and just beginning, and when both people are looking to the other for their cues, well, I now know how fragile it is. How delicate and uncertain. How it can be lost because of fear. *We are all fools in love.*

We never really come back from that. There are the occasional moments of courage, but we never figure out how to be courageous at the same time. Jack meets my unkindness with his own a month later when I run into him on the subway platform. I walk up to him to say hello and he glances at me, a mumbled *hey* casually tossed in my direction before turning away, totally engrossed in the phone in front of him. I am mortified, deeply wounded. The next day at work I barely meet his eyes when he comes over to say hello. He turns on his heel and walks away with his head tilted ever so slightly upwards, one hand rubbing the back of his neck. We are both, occasionally, tremendously and wildly ungenerous.

We do get close. There is muted flirting over email, the time in July he invites me to the bar across the street, the moment he asks where I am headed and I manage not to say, or when he grabs my waist at the concert, but doesn't hang on. And yet there is never enough to assure us of the other's affection. And as many times as he turns his head to look at me before getting on the elevator, or as many times as I walk into the kitchen hoping he'll follow, it is simply not enough. It was always going to require a leap.

When I leave that job, months later, we agree we'll grab a drink. But when he comes to chat about a date, his boss walks out from one of the conference rooms and we both get flustered, and he says, *We'll figure it out*, as he begins a slow retreat. *Well, you know, only if you want to*, I call out after him, which is the part of the story that when I tell the men in my life they always drop their heads into their hands, shaking them back and forth with a slow exhale. When I leave work that day, for the last time, Jack stands ten feet away from me, his eyes barely meeting mine as he says *Goodbye* and *See you around* and *Best of luck* like we aren't even friends. Which, I suppose, we aren't.

I regret little I've done in my life. Given the chance to go again, there are of course things I'd do differently, but I regret so little. I am not sorry that I never told the first man I loved that I did in fact love him, and I am not sorry for the mess of the others—all of the mistakes and missteps in between. But occasionally when I think about if I've ever really made a man smile—or if I ever might—Jack's name sticks at the back of my throat. And my fear is that I never gave him a smile to equal that. *That* is my great regret—that I didn't look at him in a way that said, *You are enough. You with your kind eyes and confident stride and inexplicably messy hands are exactly, totally, thrillingly right. And there is not one thing you could do to make that not true for me.*

Sometimes now, when I'm most lonely, I'll offer up a small and quiet prayer. Three words. *A man's hands, a man's hands, a man's hands*, and it is Jack who I think of.

WEST 4TH STREET

There is a moment, walking out of the subway together, just after I catch up to him, when from the corner of my eye I watch Jack quickly smooth down his hair—three quick flicks of the wrist, his head turned ever so slightly so as to hide the gesture. It is not a relaxed, cool-guy hair-swoop, it is the gesture of a boy who has been caught unprepared. *Oh, you too*, I think. Because it is in this way, his hand to his hair, that he gives himself away. And if I weren't already in love with him, I would be now, for this alone.

THOMPSON STREET

I am a week away from a visit to Boston the first time my brother mentions her. She is a new friend, a recent addition to his group. My brother has invited me to attend a formal party and so texts a picture of Caroline in a black cocktail dress. *Something like this*, he says, ever the big brother. *Yes, I know what evening wear looks like*, I respond, laughing.

I end up wearing a white tulip dress with a halter neckline that I got for 60 bucks at a vintage shop in Brooklyn. I wear it with a thin gold belt that the store owner had slipped off her own waist in favor of my own. *It'll be perfect*, she had said. And it is. Except the bottom of the skirt tapers such that I can't take long strides and so end up having to walk with great care. My brother teases me about my slow pace as we make our way to the restaurant. *I worry for the man who has to put up with you*, he says.

I laugh with him, but quietly swallow the fear that there is some truth in this—that there is something about me that is simply too much, and that I am, fundamentally, not worth the trouble. We sit next to one another at dinner, my brother on my left, Caroline on my right. I like her right off the bat. She is charming and outgoing. She flirts well and easily—with everyone—new friends and old friends and the guy at the table next to us who she has met only minutes before. She is so very much all of the things that do not come easily to me.

There are others at the table, all part of the same group of friends. There is the boy across from me who made millions straight out of college by working for an investment banking firm. He is one of the funniest people I have ever met, and one of the saddest, too. By the end of the night, too many beers in, he is cruel in that way that some men are as they attempt to flirt, his hurt suddenly so naked that I have to look away. He is half in love with a thin, blonde woman at the other end of the table who has graduated from college only some months before and is dating a boy in London who rarely comes to visit. And then there is the guy who sits at the head of the table, his floppy hair and slow smile such that girls standing nearby can't help but turn and look. He has mastered the art of looking up from beneath his fringe, his head half-cocked, the start of a smile like a perpetual invitation. He is uncommonly attractive, but it seems to me he has a secret that will take him years to share, if ever. Altogether these friends make up an imperfect group, the sum of which is deeply appealing.

I eat cheese as my main course and drink too much wine, and when we get to the party I dance with men I've not met before and spend most of the evening laughing, half-drunk on wine and happiness. Just after midnight I pull off my tights in the bathroom of the bar we've moved to, and at two in the morning we all trek up a steep hill at the back end of Beacon Hill, four boxes of pizza between us, our finest dress clothes in various stages of disarray, my bare legs shivering against the January air, joy or something like it pressing in close.

Are you dating her? I ask my brother the next morning.

No, no, we're just friends, he responds quickly.

Caroline had worn the black dress from the photo. She had the lightest hair I'd ever seen and was pretty, but not exceptionally so, which shouldn't matter, but did, because it mattered to her.

Will you ever? I ask.

No, I'm not attracted to her, he says without turning his head to look at me, flicking through the channels in an endless, careless rotation. But she is always around. Lounging on his couch, texting at odd times. A year later, on the first night we all meet my brother's girlfriend, Caroline is the person she seems most surprised and delighted to meet.

Caroline moves from Boston to New York the following November, and on a weekend in March when my brother is in town, she joins us out at a bar and tells us how the guy she's been subletting from has asked her to find a new place to live by the end of the month. She tosses her hair behind her, laughs, and says he's dumped her as a roommate. I don't think much of this at the time; living situations are always hard in New York, and finding someone with whom you can live is often impossible.

Many good friendships have been doomed by such close proximity.

My lease is up in June, I say. *We can look for a place together.*

And so it begins.

I am in the middle of a very bad year. I have just switched jobs and my heart is breaking daily for a man who does not love me. New York feels impossible—all of the dreams I moved here for are either lost or still out of reach, and so I convince myself that this small apartment will make a difference.

Manhattan is never cheap, but we are looking at a time of the year when it is particularly expensive. And I am leaving my beloved studio apartment in Brooklyn for one reason and one reason alone: a lower rent. Because Caroline works across the river in New Jersey we are limited by location—we need to find something close to the train that crosses beneath the Hudson River.

We go one day to see a first-floor duplex in Chelsea. It is too expensive and the realtor—a former model and son of some very famous drummer I've never heard of, who has the most impressive body odor I've ever encountered—lies to us right off the bat about the cost of his commission. Having lived in New York for ten years, such blatant dishonesty and clear manipulation is high on my list of things I no longer have time for. And the apartment isn't worth it, neither the layout nor location are worth the cost. The next day Caroline messages me to say that she thinks we should take it—she and the former-model-son-of-a-drummer have been texting, and he has convinced her it is a great deal. I hold my ground and instead find a lovely and small two-bedroom apartment on the Lower East Side with exposed brick and exquisite cabinetry. *Too far from the train*, Caroline responds. We look at high rises in the Financial District—one-bedroom apartments split in half by flimsy temporary walls, and proper two-bedrooms in the West Village that would eat the whole of my yearly salary.

We finally find a place at the end of April. We are both ready to be done with the search, and as it is a proper two-bedroom we call it a win. We all toast the event with vodka—the landlord, Caroline, and I—in the basement of a building just up the road. There are so many warning signs, but I gloss over them and we move in on the first of May—because that is what Caroline needs—which means I have to break my lease in Brooklyn a month early. I do it on the grounds that I have had mice for the better part of a year, which is true, but as the fight with the landlord doesn't resolve for another eight months, it proves hard and ugly and not totally worth it. Caroline takes the larger room in the new apartment on Thompson Street and I let her.

The first sign of trouble is the look on Caroline's mother's face when she sees the space for the first time while we are moving in. I write this off as her not yet having had a child live in New York; she just doesn't know, I comfort myself. Up close the city is almost always an experiment in making concessions. But when my father visits two weeks later, the space fully furnished, and a similar look of panic clouds his eyes, I know we are in trouble.

The building is simply too crowded, too old, and too poorly managed. The trash is lofted such that it sits just below our living room window, and whenever I take the garbage out after dark I hear the scurry of small rodents. The kitchen consists of a sink and two cabinets, and time and again I come home to the smell of gas because the pilot light has gone out. The bathroom is such that my knees nearly touch my chin as I sit on the toilet. There is no place for the toilet paper and so it floats around the bathroom, resting mostly on the lip of the tub. There is an odd and constant shuffle of people on the first floor of the building which suggests the super is running some sort of business that, while not sinister, is almost certainly illegal. Later I learn that other businesses exist on higher floors—the sort that you don't ask questions about. Perhaps it all could have been manageable for a time—a good story for a later date—but when six weeks after moving in I wake with a fine line of bites just north of my hip bone, I think, *The pretending is over now.*

I call the building manager and am told that it is my fault—they've never had bedbugs in that unit before. *Never before*, he tells me over the phone.

But the guy in the apartment next door tells me that the young couple who lived there before us had them a few years back. And he and his mother a year after that. How he once went to fix his mother's flickering lamp and found hundreds of them lining the wiring.

Seven small bites just above my left hip bone. Angry and red and all in a row.

I am afraid to sleep in my bed and so purchase an air mattress and sleep on the small patch of floor between living room and kitchen. I wake in the middle of the night and still half asleep grab at my neck. I count seventeen bites in the morning as I stand in front of the small bathroom mirror, red welts splattered across my chest and neck. Caroline takes one look at me, twists her lips, turns on her heel, and walks back into her bedroom. The next night I cover myself in Vick's VapoRub because I read somewhere that they are turned off by the smell. I wake at two in the morning delirious from the heat—it is the middle of June—and quickly plunge myself into a cool tub of water. I spend the rest of the night sleeping upright in an armchair, half-shaking. The glamor of New York is never-ending.

Caroline doesn't believe me. She is not bitten, or is not allergic to the bites, and so sees it as my problem and not hers. The thing about bedbugs is they choose one person. Attracted as they are by the scent of hormones, one person usually "smells" better than the other. Of course, she doesn't know this—has no interest in knowing this—and resentment grows like a weed between us. We argue one night when she says she is tired of living out of trash bags, which is what one must do when dealing with bedbugs. She tells me she is frustrated by having to put in this effort. I point out that I too am exhausted, and looking right at me she says, *When I say "I," I mean "we."* I suck my breath between my teeth.

I make a mistake towards the middle of August, two and a half months into the bedbug debacle. My friend Greg is visiting from New Zealand. He is perhaps my oldest friend in the world—was best friends with my brother before I was even born. His visit has been on the books for many months. Even before moving in together I had let Caroline know that he'd be staying with us. She is meant to be away in South America, but instead has changed her dates and will only be gone the first two nights. I am unsure where Greg should sleep. The plan was the air mattress on the living room floor, but as my own air mattress adventure led to seventeen bug bites, I am deeply wary. Instead, I decide without asking Caroline that he can sleep in her bed for the first two nights. We'll figure it out after that. We place freshly laundered sheets on her bed, removing the comforter, and use one of my pillows. Greg only goes in there to sleep.

The second night Caroline arrives home at three in the morning. By some not so small grace, Greg hears her and calls out and we quickly strip her bed and he joins me in my room because decorum and social norms be damned. When we unspool the sheets the next night, and place them on my bed, a small bug crawls out from them, which makes me think the problem is more prevalent in her space than she is letting on—or realizes, I suppose. I apologize immediately, by email, as we are mostly keeping separate schedules and barely speaking, and I know it is too little and too late.

I am absolutely in the wrong, I know this. But I also know it is not an end-of-the-world action: this is New York and occasional shuffles are made and boundaries are blurred. I have slept on unusual sofas and in the beds of strangers, and I know that when I have been away my bed has been offered to others.

But Caroline wants to blame me for the bedbugs and because she cannot, she points to her bed and declares the sky is falling. This is the first thing that I have actually done wrong and she clings to it as unforgivable. She doesn't hate that Greg slept in her bed, she just hates me.

We fight on a day in late August, a week into my terrible job. She tells me my actions have broken her trust. And then demands that I get rid of all of my furniture because she's done. She says this as she leans back in her armchair, crossing her arms, a smug twist of the lips. My hands shake, by body seethes, and as I become increasingly upset, she grows calmer in direct proportion, which is crazy-making. It is not an attempt to make the situation better, so much as a manipulative tactic to make me feel unseen and unheard. I want to point out that she is hardly dealing with them at all, which may very well be part of the problem. Instead I hit the wall of my bedroom because I am tired and angry and this is most likely where the little suckers are living. Bedbugs, as a rule do not live only in beds, so her fixation on this point is wildly frustrating because it highlights a gross lack of understanding. She then looks me straight in the eye and accuses me of making it all up for attention.

It's a terrible thing when a person makes you doubt your own mind.

With a glass of water in one hand I calmly wonder if things will be made better if I throw the water at her. I decide against it. It comes from a deep need to reveal her humanity—a suspicion that I can shock her into revealing an emotion that is true and not simply for effect. I want something, anything, to shake her into having a normal, honest response. We fight, hurling nasty insults at one another. I say things that can never be taken back—I know this, and I am okay with it. Our friendship is done, and I am deeply, resolutely ready to excise this person from my life.

I think Caroline hates her job and hates the city and hates me, too. And I think the bedbugs have brought all of this to the surface in a way that is deeply uncomfortable for her. I understand this. But as opposed to facing any one of those disquieting feelings within herself, she has projected them all onto me. It is easier to hate me than to grapple with her sadness and frustration and the fact that New York isn't all that she hoped for. (Spoiler

Alert: *it never is*. Even when it is exceptionally good, it refuses to yield to expectations.) My girlfriend Mary kindly points out that Caroline probably doesn't even realize her anger isn't really about the bed—that for her to understand that would require a level of self-awareness she just doesn't have.

We are all of us guilty of telling ourselves lies to make our current realities easier. For many years I convinced myself that life would be better when I became thin. And then I got thin and nothing was easier. And suddenly I was face-to-face with all of the things that the lie had previously held at bay. Which was when the real work began. Sometimes I think of Caroline waking up the morning after I moved out, the moment she realized that life was no better—that she was still the same person—that everything was mostly unchanged, and I actually feel a little sorry for her.

She ends up with one of my photo albums. That's the thing about bedbugs. You wrap everything up in black, industrial strength garbage bags, and so much of what is not thrown out gets shuffled and misplaced. I would have just had her toss it, clean break and all that, but it contains photos from my parents' wedding, and a picture of my brother and myself as children. Baptisms and graduations. Real 4×6 prints of days we'll never again live. I had put it together the summer after graduation. I slipped all of my favorite photos into one place so that on the days when sadness was more present than not, I could take it off of a shelf and hold a sort of happiness between my hands. And so, I ask for it back. And ask again. I send emails. And make phone calls. I offer to pick it up.

Nearly four months after moving out, I finally go to get it from her new apartment. I walk south along the western edge of Central Park and ring the buzzer, waiting in her new lobby. A man I've never seen before brings it down, looks me square in the eye, *Are you Meg?* I nod and he hands me the book and then wordlessly turns and walks away.

I send her a message: *Thank you.*

She responds: *Yup.*

A month later I pass them on the street. We are all so busy avoiding puddles made by the melting snow that we don't see each other. It is only as we pass that I look up. I have to stop, pull off to the side and turn around and look again—my heart slamming against my ribs, everything in me suddenly alight with fear and anger. There is no one I dislike more. And no feeling I find more terrifying than this anger. I watch as she reaches for his hand and he pulls her in. He looks strikingly like my brother, just a bit rounder in the face.

Bedbugs are ridiculous. In the face of really terrible conflict and disease and mass destruction, they are nothing. And yet, there is this look that people give you when you tell them that you have them (or have had them) that's incredibly alienating. Anyone can get them, it's no one person's fault—it has nothing to do with cleanliness or clutter. And while most people understand this on an intellectual level, it doesn't stop them from attempting to rationalize why one person gets them and another does not. Because with that rationalization comes a sense of security. Never mind that it's all an illusion.

What strikes me now, after the fact, is that Caroline was only kind and charming to those in a position to give her something. She'd be lovely to the bartender, but never to the young boy who delivered her take-out. Her kindness was always a means to an end. I wonder what it is she wanted from me, and at what moment she realized I wouldn't be able to give it to her. She didn't think I flirted well and found me exhausting, and that may be true, but the thing is, the core of me is not cruel, and that, at least, is something.

AVENUE OF THE AMERICAS

I'm making a list of things I'm not allowed to say:
That I'm lonely. And that I fear this loneliness will crush me, slowly and by degrees.

That I'm in mourning for all of the lives I'm not living. And that occasionally I feel like I'm failing all of the time, and in all ways.

That there have been whole swaths of time in my life when everything I said was bracketed by apology: I'm sorry. *Yes, I can do that.* I'm sorry. *Yes, let's grab coffee.* I'm sorry. *I don't really know what I'm doing.* I'm sorry. I'm sorry, I'm sorry, I'm sorry.

That it feels like I'm stuck behind a glass wall watching everyone else live a life I've only ever dreamt of. That it is isolation in plain sight.

That I'm afraid it may never happen—that this thing that people assure me will most definitely happen may not. Unlikely, yes, but unlikely things happen every day.

That I have become greedy for affection. And I fear there is some threshold for loneliness that should I pass I may never recover. That it sometimes rushes in like a tidal wave, flooding levees and toppling internal infrastructure, leaving me at a crowded dinner table afraid to look up from my plate for fear that someone may see the sadness in my eyes.

That loving someone does make everything a little bit easier. There is this construct in psychology called trans-active memory. It is the idea that we store information and ideas—memories even—in the minds of the people around us. I cannot help but wonder if this is true of joy and sadness too? If it is possible to share emotion in this way? And what must it feel like when a person you love carries your heaviness, if only for a moment?

That there is exposure in living one's life alone.

And that for a stretch of time I walk north on Sixth Avenue each morning and pass a man who spends the whole of his day yelling upwards at the sky. I wonder if we aren't more alike than not. It would be easy to say, *No, of course not*. But, loneliness, stripped of the many layers in which we dress it, is fundamentally the same.

THE D TRAIN

What if I never see him again? I ask Mary one evening on the phone.

She says that such a thing, in a long life, is more unlikely than not. The next week, while descending the subway steps, I find myself in just the right sequence of wind tunnels, with a coffee in one hand and my purse in the other, and suddenly my skirt is around my neck. And—of course—there he is, Jack, at the bottom of the stairs, waiting for the train and staring at the exposed flesh of my thighs. I regard this as a very particular blessing because the thing about the man who undoes you seeing your less-than-flattering underwear is that the worst thing has now already happened. So, I am suddenly free not to worry about my personal ineptitude when it comes to flirting.

It happens again three weeks later. Not the skirt-around-the-neck so much as the run-in. And then again a week after that. I begin to lose count. There is the time Jack is at the bottom of the stairs and I am at the top. The time he gets on after work and is reading the *Financial Times* and his glasses are tilted just so, and I am as breathless and unskilled around him as ever before.

The second time we see each other is on a Monday morning and we are meant to have drinks that Wednesday.

I see him coming down the stairs and I look at him, mute and expectant and terrified. He doesn't meet my eye as he reaches the platform, and then walks in the other direction. Later my girlfriends will tell me that he probably didn't see me, but I know. I know by the way he lifted his hand to scratch at an invisible itch. I know because I know him. Because I am proficient in the body language of playing-it-cool when you are anything but. I ride the train to work with my back to him so as to out-pretend. The date never happens, something comes up—I know before he even sends the email to say. Anne Carson writes, "To feel anything deranges you. To be seen feeling anything strips you naked."[5]

At some point, I lose count of how many dates we have set up before he cancels each one. My girlfriends begin to look at me when I talk about him with that silent and measured look that says, *He doesn't love you, move on*, but they are kind enough not to say these words out loud, and I am silently grateful because I am not ready to hear them.

On my last morning taking the train from West 4th Street before moving uptown I run into him just as I am leaving the coffee shop—we walk together to the train. I am struggling with my purse and coffee and the sudden leak of my left eye when he turns to me. *Do you need help?* he asks. I am angled away from him, wiping

---

[5] Anne Carson, *Red Doc>* (New York: Alfred A. Knopf, 2013).

at the mascara as it makes its way down my cheek; I am only marginally less embarrassed than that time he saw my underwear.

No, no, I casually brush him off. Except that I do—I do need help—so I take a breath and turn to face him, *Actually, yes, can you hold this?*

And as I stand there, adjusting my bags and wiping my eye, I watch as Jack places the lid back atop my coffee, his hands tan and weathered, gently pressing the lid down. It is such a small thing. And yet, I don't have to ask him to do it; help is offered freely.

Months later we run into each other once more. I have sent a note just before the holidays confessing as much love as I am able, and he has written back immediately, promising coffee, when he can. I am behind him on the subway steps when I notice his charcoal coat. I catch up to him at the turnstiles and we walk out together. I let him lead. I notice he takes the path I always use, which is different than his own; it is a small kindness on his part, and I am grateful for it. It is cold and we stand on the sidewalk, just off to the side, the collars of our coats popped high against our necks, our wool hats low on our ears. It has been months since we've seen one another, but for once the smiles come easily. He begins the conversation where we last left off. *How is work? Are you still living uptown? Your family is good?* And when the inevitable quiet pause comes, that moment when someone must take a risk, I break the silence because I cannot risk being made a fool of again: *You look well. You seem really well.* He says the same and hugs me for the first time; it feels like a goodbye.

When asked for his definition of paradise, Johnny Cash said, "This morning, with her, having coffee."[6]

A returned coffee lid, an extra set of hands. A lifetime of not always having to ask. Occasionally I am rendered breathless by how much there is to look forward to.

---

[6] Johnny Cash's answer to one of the questions in *Vanity Fair*'s famous Proust Questionnaires. As quoted in *Vanity Fair's Proust Questionnaire: 101 Luminaries Ponder Love, Death, Happiness, and the Meaning of Life*, ed. Graydon Carter (New York: Rodale Books, 2009).

VINEGAR HILL, BROOKLYN

In April I stand in front of the north-facing wall of my small Brooklyn apartment, and with a paintbrush in one hand and a can of white paint in the other, I quietly sob. The realities of life in New York are occasionally crushing, and I am perpetually one set of hands short. Because the wall in front of me is large and immovable.

Yet I stand and I paint, not well, but done is better than not. And then I pack and sort, and on a rainy Saturday afternoon I load my belongings into a truck and drive east across the river and back into the city. Six months later, I sit on the floor of my tiny Greenwich Village apartment, tired and heartbroken—a friendship lost, and I do it all again. New York is dying to me and I know it.

There is a tiny neighborhood in Brooklyn, across the river, tucked high on a hill. Few people have heard of it. It is quiet and odd and not totally easy to get to. For all I can tell, it comprises a single cobblestoned street, two restaurants, and a very many trees. *Vinegar Hill.* It is my favorite place in all of New York.

It is here that I celebrate my 29th birthday in one of its two restaurants with my friend Jo and her husband.

Jo takes one look around and remarks that I have strong *Walden* tendencies, and she is right. As soon as she says it, I laugh, because of course—of course, I do! And though my friends are kind enough not to ask, the question of why I am in New York grows ever more voluble. My Thoreauvian inclinations have grown in direct proportion to the time I've spent here. Ten years. Ten years of unforgiving crowds and endless subway rides and crummy apartments and shitty landlords and still more questions than answers.

I have this dream in which I am standing on a crowded subway platform and the train is delayed; it has taken entirely too long in coming. And I think maybe, just maybe, I should leave the station and look for taxi, but I am afraid that the moment I leave the train will come.

When people do ask why I have not yet left New York, this is my best explanation. I offer it with a shrug of the shoulders and raised hands—part supplication, part prayer: because surely the train will come. And because I'm afraid that when it does, I will miss it.

The truth is I don't yet know when I will leave, or why. I don't know if when the train finally comes I will quietly wait for those on board to spill out before I slip on, or if I'll have already turned around and walked up the subway steps and into the sunlight. I really don't know. But what I do know is I will leave New York with different dreams than those with which I first arrived—smaller dreams, simpler ones: an extra set of hands; "This morning, with him, having coffee." And with the dream of *Walden*, a sort of hope carried within, dependent on neither a person nor place, "success unexpected in common hours."[7]

---

[7] Henry David Thoreau, *Walden, or, Life in the Woods*, 1st edition (Boston: Ticknor and Fields, 1854).

HARLEM

After two ill-fated moves, I end up in a house in Harlem. I move in on the second of January, alone, and in two cab rides. I lug suitcases and small boxes up three flights of steps into a small room on the fourth floor and I do my best just to breathe.

Something in me has fractured. There is a small fissure that I am afraid, should I move too quickly, will splinter and crack; I am afraid of falling into the mouth of the thing. And so, I move slowly, tentatively, am careful with myself.

I pull out loose photographs and curl painter's tape against their backsides before placing them on the wall, confident that I can remove them quickly if need be. I set mirrors and frames atop the dresser, but I never once pull out a hammer, afraid to create holes that I may later need to fill. I take up space, just not too much.

I left the apartment on Thompson Street in the middle of October on a day when the sky was that impossible autumnal blue. At the time, Caroline and I had not spoken in two months, despite sharing a small space, and she had gone home for the weekend leaving me to disappear as quietly as possible. *Don't leave in the middle of the night*, she had said to me in August, before we had our fight, and I had been caught off guard by this. As though I could disappear myself and all of my things without making any noise—as though I might. In the end it was a clunking, inelegant escape—taxi rides uptown and very much stuff left on a small stretch of curb between Bleecker and West Houston. I got rid of every piece of furniture I owned, most of it inexpensive and worn, but I kept the one small reading chair my parents gifted me on my 25th birthday. I donated what I could, but the rest—a bed, a chest of drawers, and the two mahogany end tables that belonged to my grandmother and that I had promised my father I'd look after—was left just in front of the apartment building. I had neither the space nor the energy to move anything that was not absolutely essential; I felt like a failure.

I headed to my girlfriend Leena's apartment in Midtown. She had, some months before, moved home to the mountains to marry the man she loved and so offered her space as a midway point between this very bad thing, and what would surely follow. The generosity of the offer, and the deep friendship that prompted it, were things for which I may never be able to sufficiently thank her. The only catch was I was not actually allowed to live there, so each day I smiled at the doormen and told them that I was visiting my friend, and for two and a half months we all of us lived with this lie. They kindly turned away when I showed up with too much stuff, and again, when I left with even less.

★

I arrive in Harlem, opening the cab door into January's bone dry wind, my teeth chattering, my arms tired, the bags heavy, and I stand in front of the hundred-year-old brownstone which is sandwiched between two streets most New Yorkers have never heard of. It has a stoop, an iron gate, and a tiled entryway just beyond. There is a park at the end of the street and a coffee shop around the corner. It is a house in a city where such a thing is hard to come by. I have no intention of staying for more than a few months, but I will be wrong, as I have been about nearly everything this past year.

The splintering of a friendship is a particular sort of heartache. But this feels bigger than that. Darker. And I am, at this moment, not altogether fine.

I had answered an ad. Ten years in New York and it was my first time. I sent an email at the start of December and went to look at the house a few days later. It was a share—short-term and fully furnished. Joni, who lived there permanently, sat in a large armchair on one side of the living room, and I sat across from her on the couch, my shoes off, my legs tucked beneath me, an attempt to hide the holes in the feet of my stockings. I answered her questions honestly, but without saying too much. Many times over the last year my deep impulse towards honesty had been used against me, so I didn't tell her that I'd just lost a friend—that whatever it was that once joined us had torn in some irrevocable way. I did not tell her that the worst and shakiest year of my life was just now ending. And that in losing this friend, I had lost many more—that my brother and I could no longer figure out how to speak to one another. Instead I told her I wouldn't stay long, that I planned to leave New York—I wanted to go to Europe, and then somewhere else—anywhere else, really. And while I would mean all this when I said it, none of it would prove true.

Joni has made the bed in anticipation of my arrival—clean, fresh sheets neatly folded and tucked in at the corners. The sight of this small kindness feels like coming up for air after too long underwater.

I move into the house sure I will keep to myself. I will ferry to and from work, eat quickly in the evening, and then retreat to my room. I have stopped dreaming of thick rugs and hardwood floors. Of hanging pots and granite countertops. Clean white walls and crown molding. I have let go of the idea of permanency and roots and What Comes Next. I have begun to dream instead of travel. Of leaving. Of letting go and moving on. The idea of home, in any physical sense, has become as small as a glass jar filled with coffee beans, and two winter coats: one for everyday use, the other for the occasional evening out. To allow myself to imagine anything else is to be crushed by all that I do not have—all that I have just left on the side of the curb, and all that I imagined my life would be by this moment in time. I have let go of expectations and, without meaning to, of hope, too.

This house in Harlem is alive with noise and movement—the television left on, the dissonant chords of a piano always just a bit out of tune, the shuffle of footsteps. The music of everyday life, full and good and deceptively mundane. It is so different than I had imagined. There is a working fireplace in the living room, and a full kitchen, a deck just off the side of the house. I didn't want to live with others, certainly not with strangers. How long I avoided this very situation. And yet it is here, in this *Dickensian boarding house*, as my girlfriend Alice has dubbed it, that I begin to unclench, to feel my way back to myself. It is not lost on me that as soon as I let go of the notion of home, I land in one. And for a stretch of time, a small room on the top floor of a hundred-year-old brownstone, filled with furniture belonging not to a person but a place, is my own.

There are four of us altogether. The boy who lives in the room next door is lovely and impish. Joe is studying law at Columbia and clearly brilliant, but he mostly can't remember to tie his own shoes. His door is always open and he naps in the middle of the day—sometimes in the evening, too, his mouth open, his cheeks flushed, his limbs splayed in every direction. When he is not sleeping, he is in perpetual motion—pedaling on his stationary bike, running up and down the stairs, banging away at the piano. He is his own small tornado of energy and I am grateful for his contained chaos—there is not an ounce of pretense about him. The two of us share a bathroom, and the first week I arrive he leaves a note on the mirror to say he's headed to California to escape the cold, he'll see me in a week's time—and *Oh yeah, I've cleared my shelf for you to use*, he writes. Again a small kindness, again startling.

The woman who lives down the hall, Charlotte, is away when I first arrive. Her room feels—and is talked about—as though it were the forbidden west wing of the house. I start to wonder if it contains a rose quietly losing its bloom beneath a bell jar.

Quite early on I let slip to Charlotte and Joe that I have recently had bedbugs, and they smile and nod, and take that nearly imperceptible step away from me, which is understandable, but still isolating.

For the first two months, I talk around the subject of why I left Greenwich Village with Joni. I tell her that a friend and I have had a rough go of it, and she smiles and listens. And then finally, when I can take it no longer, as we stand in the kitchen one Sunday afternoon I say, *There is something I haven't told you, and I want you to know I took all of the necessary precautions, and please keep in mind that I lived somewhere else before coming here, but the thing about the apartment on Thompson Street—the thing that precipitated the fallout with Caroline—well, we had bedbugs.*

Okay, she says, without even shifting the weight on her feet.

Okay? I ask.

Yeah, I'm not worried about it. I don't think we'll get them, but if we do, we'll deal with it.

Joni is so unfazed by what I have to say, and her lack of a response proves the most remarkable thing anyone has done for me in the last stretch of several months. Something in my chest begins to soften.

Charlotte, who is nearly 30 years my senior, gives me a green notebook early on, to encourage me to write. She suggests we wake early to walk through the park. She invites me out to a bar with the young guy she is working with. Eventually I am invited to pass the threshold of her room to the space within. It is massive, with a working fireplace, and we sit in there on more than one occasion drinking wine in front of the fire as we chat or work or watch old films.

It is probably two months before I realize that something is not quite right. I have found there are two sorts of people in the world—those who have been through the shit, and those who have not. And this first group, their particular shit, well it either turns them kind or else shrinks their world in a way that makes them cruel. Charlotte, I discover, is the latter; she is not nice, and cannot be wrong. She dresses her cruelty in such fine manners so as to make it hard to detect. She is strangely interested in what I look like—what do I use on my hair and my skin, and what clothes do I wear? She attempts to set me up with her young colleague and I demur, as he has had the same girlfriend for going on a decade. I begin to notice the story she tells about me and this man is one in which I have no agency, so I smile and nod and try to hide my deep frustration before changing the subject. I suspect that she is actually half in love with him, something about him reminding her of the husband she lost many years before. One day I bring home dresses from the store and she eyes them before asking what size they are. I think this is an odd question, but check the tags and answer. She chuckles softly and says in her lilting Australian accent, *Oh, you Americans and your vanity sizing.*

One night while speaking in the kitchen Charlotte asks about my future and where I'll settle down, and I say it'll depend in part on who I end up with, and she laughs to herself—at me, about me—and says, *Oh dear, you sound like a Brontë sister.* It is intentionally cruel. It doesn't feel like the appropriate moment to explain that the Brontë sisters were early feminists in how they wrote about partnerships, by far outpacing their male counterparts, and is it so terrible to sound like one? A month later, when I bring a quiet and lovely boy named John to a party at our house, she asks about Jack, with whom I am desperately in love and desperately trying to get over, and in whom she'd shown no previous interest discussing because *Wasn't it clear that he just wasn't interested?* Now it is me who begins to back away, quietly, slowly. Something has soured and we both know it.

Joe moves out of the house at the end of May upon graduation from law school. He has a very good job waiting for him at a prestigious law firm someplace with warmer winters. Charlotte is meant to leave at the same time, as her current job has ended, but is delayed by several weeks. A man is going to take her room, which will help balance the house dynamic. A woman named Emily moves into the room next to mine. She is in her late thirties, a television producer, and has several weeks off before her next job. For a month and a half, we are four grown women all living together, which smacks of Miss Havisham.

Emily is fine for a grand total of five days before she turns odd and quiet. She slams her door and jangles her keys so as to signal her arrival home. If she leaves her room for more than a minute she'll lock the door behind her, as though one of us might just pop in there and take something. If I am in the living room with Joni, she's polite and inclusive, but if I am alone, or on the steps behind her, she pretends I'm not there. It is fascinating and more than a little crazy-making. She removes her things from the bathroom three months before moving out, and for the last two, the only sound that comes from her room is that of packing tape. Once, while we are both in the kitchen, I notice the stove is still on and ask if I can turn it off, and she reaches across the burners without taking her eyes off me, and I swear I can see her sneer.

For the six weeks Emily and Charlotte overlap they are thick as thieves, and I sense Emily's animosity stems from this. Their relationship is mostly contained to Charlotte's room. They are both waiting for their respective next jobs to begin and so they stay in their pajamas all day and don't leave the house. Just a month after Charlotte leaves, Emily tells Joni that she'll move out at the start of November, and I am secretly thrilled.

Three days before she is set to leave I wake early to use the bathroom we both share. It is 7:15 when I walk out, wrapped in a towel, my hair dripping down my back. She is sitting on the top step, three paces away, and tells me that I was not to have entered the bathroom before half past the hour—that we'd agreed on this when she moved in. Which I know to be untrue because, having just lived through the year of Caroline, this is not something I would have agreed to. Life is too messy and unpredictable for such stringent rules. When I attempt to disagree, she begins to argue with me, and I simply say: *Emily, we have three days left living together, let's just get through this.* She seems shocked by this, and I realize that she has had no idea, until this very moment, that I was aware of her vitriol. I am reminded in that moment that self-hatred tends to fold the world in on itself, creating an echo chamber of one's own rancor. She slams the door to the bathroom behind her, calling out: *Have a great day,* again and again.

I don't sleep at home that night, opting to stay with Jo instead. There is something about Emily's particular brand of aggression that feels only moderately contained. She leaves on a Saturday night without saying goodbye.

In those first two months after moving in, when Charlotte and I were still friends, I told her the whole story of what happened with Caroline, and I felt something in her shift. She could not understand how I would have done such a thing, allowed another person to sleep in Caroline's bed. *I know, I was wrong*, I said, owning the mistake. But Charlotte could not let it go. I think this is why Emily locks her door when I am around—I think Charlotte has told her this story. And all I can do is sigh and laugh and marvel at the fallibility of humans. I was wrong, I made a mistake, but I am not a terrible person because of this one thing, right? But three women have just looked at me as though I am, and I begin to fear that maybe they are right.

A friend says to me calmly: *Some people just need an enemy.*

But why? I ask.

Because it's the only way they know they are good.

When Emily moves out, the unholy trinity of women is a circle complete.

I light sage to rid her room of any residual ugliness and then lie on the bed and send up a silent prayer that bears a striking resemblance to a deep exhalation of relief.

Charles moves into Emily's now vacant room the second week of November, and I am nuts about him from the start. It would be easy to say that I adore him in part because I so disliked—or rather, was so deeply terrified by—those who came before, but it is bigger than that. He is unusually kind. We stand in the doorframes of our two adjacent rooms at the end of each day, the washing machine going, and he asks how I am, and then waits to hear the answer. He buys me bourbon after he assures me that I'll hear back from a guy after a really great first date and I do not. He is an optimist like few I've known, and I occasionally worry he does not extend this kindness to himself.

Months later, in January, his fiancée Elle unexpectedly gets a job in New York—they are both actors—and she moves in, too. It never feels crowded. The three of us share a bathroom and we go through the toilet paper too quickly, and there is more hair to remove from the drain, but I come home every day and sit at the kitchen table and share my triumphs and deep frustrations, and I am loved in new ways. I walk home each night looking to see if their light is on, hoping it is. Our friendships form fast and hard in that living room, all of us laughing in front of the fire.

In July, I sit in the basilica on the campus of Notre Dame and watch as these two people whom I love, whom I have known for such a short time, yoke their lives to one another. I don't cry when Elle walks down the aisle, or when Charles, with shaking hands, wipes his eyes. Rather my tears come when the priest starts in on the homily and talks about tilting the mirror of our lives ever so slightly upward—to focus on and reflect all the good. And I sit there stunned by the sheer chance of this moment. That I would end up in a house in Harlem—that Joni's kindness would make a home of that place. That Charles would move in just when he did, and Elle just after. I am astonished by what the mirror is reflecting back.

Charles and Elle move out just before their wedding, back to Los Angeles, and I move into their larger bedroom with its three windows and stone fireplace and queen-size bed.

I paint slowly over many days. The walls turn blue, steadily. The color is darker than expected, but it grows on me. I was wooed by the name of it in the paint shop: Santorini Blue. Which helps, for a moment, to stave off the wanderlust. Europe never did happen for me—at least, not in the way I expected. Instead my mother and I spent ten days in Paris and Barcelona, and in the course of that short time I felt something in me shift and I knew there would be no turning back. That my time sitting at a desk for ten hours a day working on projects with little meaning would be limited.

I paint the moulding white, the windowsills too, which opens the whole room up. I put down painter's tape and peel it away again when the paint has dried. It is slow going and the whole process is a sort of experiment in feeling my way back to myself. I pull out a hammer and nails, and make holes in the wall for pictures and shelves. I begin to take up space. It's been a year and a half since that second day in January, two years since I left the apartment in Brooklyn, desperately painting a dark wall white so that no one would know I'd ever been there.

There is something about the proximity and persistence of the way in which I have been cared for in this house, that is nearly disorienting. Elle, a force of nature, proves to be the friend I didn't know I needed. She is ferociously loyal and unapologetically feminine. She is ballsy in a way that is both startling and awe-inspiring. I watched her for the six months we all lived together and thought, *Me too, I can be that too*. Before she moved in, I worried that I'd lose my burgeoning friendship with Charles; instead we became a family complete—Charles, Elle, Joni and me sitting around the dinner table arguing politics, and laying bare our hopes for the future.

Not once do they suggest I "sound too much like a Brontë" to be reasonable. They tell me Jack was just not my guy, and whoever is will be worth the wait. They assure me that nothing is wrong with me—that I love well and am deserving of good things, and that it's okay to want to share my life with someone. In fact, the night after their wedding, in a bar in the middle of Indiana, Elle grabs my arm firmly, and looks me right in the eye: *Don't you dare settle, Meg. Don't you dare. He's coming and holy hell will he be worth the wait.* For as long as I live I will never forget that moment. The smell of the bar, the floor sticky beneath our feet, and the look in Elle's eyes.

Just two months after their wedding, Elle goes to a doctor with dull, pulsing pain in her breast. Cancer. She waited her whole life to find Charles—38 years—and two months after pledging the rest of it to him, she gets a diagnosis. *In sickness and in health.* Dammit. But there is no way to protect against that which is difficult, and so we continue on. And we fight for what we want, and we fly across the country, and we prioritize what has meaning and we show up for those we love. And we remember that that which is broken is also holy. We tilt the mirror up.

Five months after Charles and Elle move out of the house and home to LA, I board a plane to surprise them. Joni is already there visiting, and she arrives at their gate on a sunny Sunday morning and rings their bell. Elle comes out and they chat for a moment, and then Joni mentions that she's brought something for them. I step forward and Elle begins to cry, asking again and again, *Is this real?* The three of us hug and my heart is so full with these women. That night we sit around their dining room table eating pizza and arguing politics, the election looming, and Elle begins to laugh, her head bent. *I've missed this*, she says, looking at us, her eyes bright and full.

I could never have imagined that in answering an ad I'd find these people who would redefine and reshape my understanding of community. Who would fight for me and cry with me and argue about the merits of skim milk versus whole. Who would loan luggage and champion my worth and make New York less lonely. These people who would love me, mess of disparate wants that I am.

Home found where it was least expected. And hope returned.

EAST 48TH STREET

It ends with John's warm beer on the table—only half drunk, him having chosen his words carefully.

We just weren't a match, I say, trying to make it okay. Trying to make what feels slippery in our mouths less so. John seems more terrified than I feel, and I really want to make this okay for him.

We sit in silence for a few beats, in a dark midtown pub that smells of stale beer and aging men, his light brown eyes on the bottle in front of him. A man at the bar sits with his body angled towards me, one eye on the television, the other on me; John doesn't notice. I suggest we leave—he doesn't like his beer, no use in forcing him to drink it. We push back our chairs, the floor sticky beneath us, and—barely looking at one another—hug uncomfortably. I walk west, he goes east.

I've always thought of the east side of New York as a terribly lonely place.

There was no white horse, no dazzling suit of armor, just his soft voice and quiet footsteps. His kind eyes and slow, deliberate smile. I spent those first few months watching him, wondering what to make of him, suspended in a thick, buoyant tangle of my own ambivalence.

To fall in love or not, as though it were a question that could be answered by thinking alone.

We were introduced by friends. On our first date, he said something about *Walden* and I thought, *Oh, well, there's that*. I had no intention of liking him. And so the *Walden* thing—his respect and appreciation for Thoreau and the wilderness—felt inconvenient.

Everything about John was a surprise, my affection for him most of all. And how he chose to end it—that was a surprise too. We were fine, and then we were busy, and then we were not fine.

He ended it over the phone. He sent a small text, four words: *We need to talk*. I knew what it meant without him having to say, but he suggested we meet in person, and I agreed because I thought that to want the intimacy of a relationship was to accept the uneasy intimacy of breaking up.

Days later, over different beers with different people, he would use my words as a way of an explanation. He would say, *We just weren't a match*, and someone would relay this to me. And my heart would break just a little because, although they were my words, that wasn't my experience. Or, well, it was at the very least more complicated than that.

Perhaps there is more I should have said, sitting at that small table, with warm, bad pub drinks between us. About doubt and how it is a thing that multiplies in the absence of a warm hand or the sound of a person's laugh or a quiet, full look. How it grows, alone in silence on sleepless nights, or under the unrelenting glare of another's comments. How it is a nasty trick of fear. And we were both so busy.

But it is not my job to convince a man to love me. It cannot be my job to convince a man to love me.

It's just that he made everything easier, for a moment. And for a moment I felt hopeful.

I won't say I miss him, even though I do, because it feels like there is a limit to the grief we can afford when the relationship was barely a thing. And it's not so much grief as an occasional dull ache, and I don't know how much of that ache is him, and how much is just life.

I was not in love with John. It's just that every time I walked out my front door and saw him standing on the sidewalk looking up at me, I'd think, *This is a man I like walking towards*. And that was not nothing.

Most days I'm okay. But then I'll be out running errands and a memory will come quickly, quietly. It's always the little things. The wristband of his watch. The book he'd carry in the front pocket of his jacket. His dark brown hair just after a cut. How occasionally he'd remove his glasses, take a breath, and smile as if he was just catching up to himself, his cheeks pink and full beneath the stubble. And for a moment—for just a moment—I'll miss the time it took to cross the nine steps between my front door and where he stood on the sidewalk below.

118TH STREET

I walk home breaking off small pieces of the dark choco-late bar in my purse. It is snowing. It is the first day of spring and it is snowing. I don't mind; it quiets the world, slows things down.

I have been homesick all winter long, but can't quite place the feeling, as the city has been home for so long that how can I be homesick when I am already here? Perhaps it's more of a longing for permanence, which still feels so maddeningly elusive.

From a block away I see the windows in my brown-stone lit up. *That's the feeling*, I think. The sensation of walking towards home—of being nearly there. The lit window, the cool night, the smell of a wood fire in the air. I'm not sick for home so much as the promise of it, a block away. The knowledge that I'm nearly there.

NORTH SALEM

We drive around the back roads of North Salem, his truck struggling up the steep hills. We are an imperfect match, but I am okay pretending for a bit. The problem comes when I forget this is only meant to be make-believe. My chin rests on my hand, my elbow against the window, the bucolic countryside whirring past. It is finally spring and the late afternoon light makes the trees and water appear as though they are lit from within. He asks me what I want—what I really want—and I get a little quiet because I'm not sure how to say it.

Freedom and stability, I utter moments later, without turning to look at him. I can hear him thinking, but he says nothing.

What does that mean? John finally asks.

Trips to Europe, I think. *The moment the music breaks its pattern. The hang-time just before a basket is made—that split-second suspension. Edith Piaf on the record player and thunderstorms in the summer. A very big life*, I think, *made up of the very small things.*

I don't say this to him. Instead I mumble something and we both fall silent.

You have so many opinions, John had once said to me. I always thought this was a good thing, but the way he said it in that moment made me think he felt differently.

There is a study by Cutler and Scott that shows when women speak for a fourth of the conversation, they are perceived by men as taking up half of it; I glance sideways at John sitting in the front of the truck and wonder if he feels this way.

For a moment, I revisit the old lies I used to tell myself. Perhaps if I am physically smaller, I can take up more space, have more opinions, be a bit more vocal in what I believe. I know this is wrong. On an intellectual level, I know this is wrong, that life doesn't really work this way, and yet I still think about it for longer than I care to admit.

I want a life that cannot be plotted on spreadsheets or graphs. I want to get married in the mountains, with flowers in my hair, and a prayer in my eyes. I want to stand in front of God and the sky and do something common and brave. I want to stay up until three in the morning arguing about politics and drinking too much whiskey, and then to crawl into bed, placing my head on the man's chest, and fall asleep without moving. And then I want to wake and do it all over again the next day.

John is never going to look at me like he is in love with me. And I am never going to look at him like I am in love with him. And we are both searching for different *Waldens*, sitting in the front of his truck watching different landscapes unfurl before us.

57TH AND THIRD

Even in the darkest moments—or especially then—it always seemed to me that recovery would be measured by a distance from fear. Or that health would be the ability to hold fear in one hand and hope in the other—to balance those opposing forces.

I sat in a bar tucked just off of one of the busiest streets in Williamsburg with a girl I'm now no longer friends with. It was closer to midnight than not, but she ordered an iced coffee. With soy milk. And an extra glass of ice. And more milk. And a straw. Each request coming quick on the heels of the other, driven by what appeared to be a low-level but pressing panic. I ordered a single glass of white wine, barely meeting the bartender's eyes, and then he did what he could to avoid us for the rest of the night.

She arranged the glasses in front of her, shuffling their order, once, twice, and then once more. Fear parading as ritual.

I'm well. I'm well now, she assured me. *Healthy*.

I thought of *Hamlet*, Act 3, Scene 2: "The lady doth protest too much."

Eating disorders are funny things; the people who suffer from them dress them up and conceal them in all different manners. But like the Emperor's New Clothes, where health is concerned, they tout luxury and depth, when there's just nothing there. I was never so unhealthy as when I singularly pursued health in the name of thinness—or was it thinness in the name of health?

It was never lost on me, even when I was most unwell, that the desire to change my body was the least interesting thing about me.

It took me two years to get a diagnosis. Because starving gave way so quickly to overeating and because the disease came with a whopping incident of depression, the illness itself was a conundrum. *You're sad*, doctors would say. *It's anxiety. Take care of those things and the eating will sort itself.* And I'd stare at the small antidepressants in my hand wondering whether the chicken or the egg came first. But somehow I knew the doctors were wrong—knew that this was more specific, less ambiguous, and more dangerous than just sadness. I remember going to see a therapist in my first year at college and telling her that I couldn't sort out the image reflected back at me in mirrors. *Well, are you fat?* she responded. *I didn't get a good look at you when you walked in.* As though it had anything to do with what I looked like. I never saw her again.

When you get better, people ask you what you ate. Which is really their way of asking how you lost the weight. It always strikes me as the wrong question.

Ask me what I do and how I fill my days, and I will tell you stories of dinner with girlfriends in which we eat burgers and Brussels sprouts and baked pretzels with spicy mustard. I will speak of late night treks up steep hills, and boxes of pizza between us. I will tell you how on Christmas Eve I sit with my family at my parents' home, eating pear and blue cheese flatbread, olives and salami, and brie smeared on crackers. I will tell you of an afternoon early this year when I went to see a movie with friends and they brought a bottle of champagne and plastic cups because Will was one of the top billed actors and they thought I might need it. I will tell you how food is a part of the story, but how love and friendship are filling in far more important ways. That there a thousand ways to feed one's self—cross-country road trips, hikes, fresh mountain air, the smell of cut grass and rain.

There was once a time I worked with a girl who didn't eat any fat. Barely any meat. Her diet consisted of vegetables, Greek yogurt, and fruit, with an occasional bag of nuts. She didn't believe in unhealthy foods—as though her disbelief made them nonexistent. This is how she got better, she assured me. This is how she made peace with the daily struggle. *We have the same values about food*, she would say to me. *We believe the same things*.

I didn't have the energy to tell her that I believe in a varied diet—full of colorful things and foods she would label "bad." That I was never so unhappy as when I carried ten almonds in a zip-lock bag at the bottom of my purse. That in fact, my biggest issue is the division of food into only two categories: bad and good. Healthy and not. Acceptable and off-limits. I didn't have the energy to take her to task when she chastised others for their "unhealthy" choices. The whole thing felt so mired in fear, and so tenuous, that I kept my mouth shut. Another woman at work told me that her daughter had had anorexia—pulled up photos on her phone to flip through. *See*, she said pointing to the sharp angles of the young girl's body. I stood there, shocked that she kept the photos on her phone, that she was showing them to me. But I noticed she never ate the bread on her sandwiches.

I sat across from a guy on a second date one time who asked me, *But don't you miss it? Don't you miss those moments when you totally overindulge?* I looked at him and smiled. I thought of grocery stores and long aisles and foods wrapped in plastic and the overwhelming terror and insatiable hunger that drove me there again and again. *No*, I said to him, returning to the fried chicken in front of me. *No, I really don't.*

People tell you that it will last forever. That there is no such thing as recovery, that there is only a daily maneuvering, a reasoned management. But even in my worst moments I knew that if such a thing were true—that if it were the only truth that had ever before existed—then I would go in search of a new truth. Because to accept such a thing would be to settle for a life that was simply too small.

There are so many steps on the road to recovery. Mindful eating and food-as-fuel eating, and countless others in between, but it's my opinion that none of these things marks the end. In fact, there is no end really, there is only the moment you decide that that particular path isn't terribly scenic and you get off. Suffering is not a prerequisite to loving one's body.

There is life after an eating disorder that has nothing to do with the eating disorder. But you have to reach in that direction. You have to be unrelenting in your pursuit of better and richer and fuller experiences in which pizza and white wine and Brussels sprouts play but a part—a really good part, but still just a part.

And fear has nothing to do with any of it. Not a damn thing.

LISPENARD STREET

Jo and I pack up her apartment quickly; there is not much to do. She sorts her clothes, swiftly dispensing with the suits from those few years when she was a lawyer. I open the windows and turn on the fan—an attempt to displace the scent of stale air, sleep, and a man who has decided he no longer wants to be a husband. The scent of sadness, too—like bad alcohol, but more acidic. The street below is noisy and unforgiving, and I hate New York in this moment.

The furniture remains, most of the photos are left on the wall. In the end she is left with only two small boxes to ship across the country, back west and home again. It is late October and we dress that night for a costume party. I am Audrey Hepburn, my hair piled high, a black dress on that feels tighter than it did the month before, which for a moment stirs an ancient fear; she is a 1950s house-wife, apron around the waist, spatula in hand—irony is a small consolation in a divorce. Costumes to pretend at happiness, or something like it. Normalcy, if nothing else. That night we return to the bed she shared with her husband, and we eat popcorn and watch bad tele-vision. Jo smiles and tells me she'll be fine, and I smile and tell her I believe her, and we fall asleep side by side because that is what friends do when the worst thing has just happened.

I don't actually know what happened, am not privy to the *why*—although, to be honest, I'm not sure she is either, which must be a particular sort of torture. I really liked her husband. From the outside looking in, it seemed as though a really nice guy woke one morning and, suddenly tired of pretending, revealed himself for who he actually is.

The next morning Jo loads her suitcase into a cab, the boxes already shipped, and I lug a bag of books she doesn't want uptown to Harlem. Sitting on the floor of my small bedroom, in the house I fled to and then fell in love with, I carefully reach for the top book. *There's an inscription in there*, she'd said to me. *Get rid of it*. There, on the title page, in her husband's careful scribble, is a small love note, simple and clear, quotidian in its affection. I tear out the page, ripping it into as many pieces as I am able. Long after the worst has been said, long after the fissure into which two people tumble has split open, a friend tears out the title page of a book and the world keeps spinning.

It was pouring rain the night Jo and I met. The bar was on the corner of West Houston and Macdougal, around the corner from where I'd recently moved in Greenwich Village. A mutual friend had introduced us over email. My umbrella offered little protection against the summer storm and I arrived half-soaked, secretly thrilled, as rainstorms rank high on my list of favorite things. We sat there with the previous ten years of our lives spread out before us for examination, so different but with the same end point, which at that moment was that shitty table in that shitty bar on the border of Soho and Greenwich Village, both of us wondering what the hell we were doing with our lives.

As Jo spoke, I couldn't help but think she had done exactly what my father quietly dreamt I might: attend graduate school, get a law degree from a prestigious university, and secure a job that demanded respect and so promised stability, or something like it. For a moment the guilt was so acute that I nearly had to excuse myself from the table. That she had done it all with a person by her side was very much a part of the conversation that night. While Jo had met her husband the first week of college, the man I fell in love with in that first week had married and then divorced someone else, and I'd been alone for what felt like forever. At the time Jo and I met, I was in love with a man who would go on to break my heart in a hundred different ways, simply by not showing up. He would take far too long to get over, and Jo would learn to stop asking about him.

Jo was two months away from leaving her position at an impressive law firm, and we both sat at that high top table in that dimly lit bar, wondering what life might be if we were to do anything else. We were both searching for meaning in a city where such a thing is often obscured by bright lights and the immediacy of money.

We've done so many of the same things, she said. *The only differ-ence is I've had a man strapped to my back the whole of that time.*

I couldn't help but think we'd done none of the same things—that when she was studying for the bar, I was working at a restaurant in midtown, wearing black dresses that were too short, and eating dinner at one in the morning standing over the kitchen sink. But this caught my ear—*a man strapped to my back*. Was that how it was supposed to feel? For a moment I feared I'd wasted too much time wanting too much.

It is almost two years to the day that we first met when Jo flies back to New York for a visit, a year after her mar-riage has ended, six months after we packed up her small one bedroom in Soho. She lives in Los Angeles now but is back for business. We sit at my kitchen table, a bottle of wine between us. We have seen each other through so much in our short time as friends. Have borne witness as things unraveled in stunning haste—a single thread pulled, collapsing parts of our lives in ways we couldn't have predicted.

Jo was the first person to tell me that I needed to leave the Greenwich Village apartment. *You cannot stay there. You must leave*, she said to me. With six months left on the lease I'd felt the need to stick it out as a form of penance for poor decisions. Never mind that I'd return home each day to a small and filthy apartment, my hands shaking as I reached the landing. Never mind that I hated the per-son on the other side of the door. Or that I'd spend most evenings walking west on Bleecker towards the river in an attempt to feel solid ground beneath my feet, to keep my mind from slipping out the back end of my body. Jo was the first person to offer me a place to stay, to assure me that I did not have to continue to live with Caroline, that I could leave the apartment and forfeit the money if I had to. She was the first person to assure me that there would be guys other than Jack—better ones. She was one of the first to say, *I see you*, and, *There are better worlds than this one, and bigger lives, and to reach for one is not a failing.*

Sitting at the kitchen table, I ask her if she ever loved her husband. *I thought I did*, she replies.

This is how a marriage ends, I think. The divorce papers have been signed and are now housed in some nondescript LA County building waiting to be processed. She is in love for the first time in her life with a man who is kind and tall, with large hands and broad shoulders—a man who never speaks ill of anyone else, which is sexy in a way that our twenty-year-old selves didn't understand. Long gone is the allure of the bad boy—our mistaken confusion of unkindness for complexity. A man can be many things, but let him be kind, first.

Jo works on Saturday morning and then we have a late lunch on a roof just north of the Flatiron Building. It is the first weekend of June and the sun is beating down, so we eat orzo and drink rosé and then take the train to Queens to celebrate the birthday of a mutual friend. We sit by the water, and I watch as dark clouds gather quickly, the Manhattan skyline suddenly cut out, made clearer by the blue and gray and green of the approaching storm. Our small group walks to a nearby bar and we sit outside under an overhang as the sky opens up, and I can't help but think of the night we met and how much has changed.

Half-soaked again, Jo and I take a taxi home across the Queensboro Bridge, the city lights blotted and sparkling through the cab window. For a moment I am as in love with New York as I have ever been; for a moment everything feels exactly right. We eat cheese and bread and slices of cured meat on my bed before falling asleep with the lights still on. If there is such a thing as love it is falling asleep in bed, safe, full of cheese and wine, and full too of passing summer storms. Jo was right of course: she was always going to be fine—we both were.

This is how you make a life, I think.

16TH STREET

I am walking north on Sixth Avenue when I hear my name.

On Thursday I had told someone I felt as though I were about to see Jack. There was no reason for suspecting I would, other than the feeling itself, which is just a quick flutter in the chest, a pressing nearness. It had happened before, and it had always—without fail—proven correct, so I'd learned to give the feeling space enough to just exist.

Two days later I hear my name and turn around to see him walking out of a deli in my direction, a longboard in one hand, groceries in the other. His sunglasses are turned around on the back of his neck, and his arms are deeply tanned.

Oh, hey, Jack. My breath catches on his name.

I once loved this man; I mostly still do. I've never told him, but he knows. Surely, he knows. He knows, right?

It has been just shy of a year since we last saw one another, our once-weekly run-ins having ended when I moved uptown and stopped taking the D train from West 4th to Bryant Park. We stand there for the better part of a half-hour, talking about nothing and everything, and it feels as close as it ever did to easy, which—when push comes to shove—is still not easy enough. Twice during the conversation he asks what I am doing that evening, and I shuffle my feet and mention a friend's birthday. When I ask him the same he says, *Nothing*, closing his lips around that word, and we both pause in the silence that follows. I am waiting for him to actually ask not what am I am doing, but if I will do something with him. Instead we live in suspense for only a moment before he shifts his feet and asks where I got the coffee in my hand, and when I answer he nods and we follow that thought for as long as we can until he thinks to ask something else, equally unimportant. How close we come and how far we then move from revealing who we actually are: two strangers who could have loved one another.

When we run out of things to say, we say goodbye and turn to walk in opposite directions. I pause for a moment, turning around, and see that he has done the same.

Sometimes I'll think about some of the men before him. On days when I'm off to a wedding or a family vacation or another important aberration from the daily norm, I'll let myself daydream of a guy and wonder if we were to have attended together how it would it have gone. Whose house would we have left from, and what would we have worn, and what would it have felt like to share a taxi to the airport with that person? But then I think of Jack, and I can't get past how his glasses sat turned around on his neck. Because to allow myself to imagine anything beyond that is simply too hard.

It's hard to explain what I felt the first moment I saw him, two years before. When we first met, I took one look at him and thought, *Oh, there you are.* How wrong I was. And how little faith he had in what we were never able to say aloud.

We plan to do something three weeks after our run-in on the corner of Sixth Avenue and 16th Street. Under the perfect blue of an October sky we are meant to finally try. So many false starts, so many emails traded, so many run-ins on the street and we've found a side door in. He will give me a longboarding lesson and I will bring him coffee as payment. We go back and forth over email and pick a day, but not a time, and in the end he never responds to my last email. A hanging question, unanswered.

It seems so ridiculous now—so foolish that I thought it might actually happen. I no longer know how many dates we had set up before he canceled each and every one at the last moment. He made a fool of me. Made a fool of the affection I felt for him.

We haven't seen each other since. I caught him once out of the corner of my eye while getting off the subway, but he was too far ahead, and so I continued on to work, wondering whether the hell this feeling would ever go away.

Jack wore a wool gray coat for special occasions, and a blue pullover every day. He was from a small town in the Northeast with a predominantly Irish Catholic population. He liked sushi, and meatball sandwiches, and was the eldest of three. He worried about his mother and loved his younger sister and spoke about a cat that his father adopted that never came out from under the couch. He didn't own a television and spent his Friday nights in, slept late on Saturday mornings. He always tapped his soda cans—two quick taps—before opening, and he took his coffee black. He liked cycling and running and playing golf.

My question is this: when you stop loving someone, what are you meant to do with all of this information? Where do you put it?

WHERE BLEECKER MEETS
UNIVERSITY PLACE

I cried in the grocery store. Standing in front of the Entenmann's donuts in the Morton Williams on Bleecker Street, I wept.

The year leading up to my 30th birthday was astonishing. Mostly in its ability to wound. It was the year of so many *What ifs* and blind curves on unlit roads. A year in which, just as soon as I thought I knew where the story was going, the ground would shift beneath my feet.

What if I'd gone to Paris with Eric? What if, on that quiet day in July, Jack hadn't left the bar before I'd gotten there? What if I'd been given the promotion at work and so not changed jobs? What if I'd not moved to Greenwich Village? It was a year of countless moments that could have altered the course. Small forks in the road, so many unanswered questions. A year of heartbreak and overwhelming loneliness that felt like a Van Gogh painting in motion. All dark colors and blurred lines and movement. Very slow movement, but movement.

But this is what I know to be true, that in the worst moments of our lives, good things happen. That, in fact, the good and bad rush in together, one somersaulting over the other. And you must be alert enough to look for both.

The thing about the eating disorder is that it always felt *of* me. Like it took root in my ribs and grew and grew and grew until there was nothing else left. Whole years of my life were defined by the moments I stood in nondescript grocery stores under the unrelenting glare of fluorescent lights in front of a donut display, attempting to talk myself off the edge. *You do not need this. You are imperfect, but still good. You are not defined by this fear and frustration and anger.* And as rational as I was, I was also, in the simplest of terms, unwell. And so I'd buy a box, sometimes two, and I'd walk the half block home and eat them. All of them. And then I'd sleep.

Standing in front of those donuts I wept because, rough as things are, I'll never again confuse some large cosmic hunger with the need for food. But I also wept because there is some part of me that mourns the loss of how I was loved during that time—I've never felt so exquisitely cared for by my family as in those darkest moments of my life. I felt their love in everything: as my mother and I leaned against scaffolding waiting for a summer storm to pass, or when my father bought me a pound of cherries from a vendor on the street. And in its purest, most uncomplicated form, that love was a force.

C.S. Lewis wrote in *The Problem of Pain*:

If God is Love, He is by definition something more than mere kindness. And it appears from all the records that though He has often rebuked us and condemned us, He has never regarded us with contempt. He has paid us the intolerable compliment of loving us in the deepest, most tragic, most inexorable sense ... it is natural for us to wish that God had designed for us a less glorious and less arduous destiny; but then we are wishing not for more love but for less.[8]

"Wishing not for more love but for less."

I was always going to choose the path in service of more love. Always. And if these years of heartbreak have been in service of that, okay then. More love it is.

Once upon a time, I counted calories and whittled my body in an attempt to make knowable that which was anything but. And then I ate a lot of food and gained a lot of weight as a way to absent myself from my own life. But no amount of food or added fat or lost hours could alter the gravitational pull of life itself—its precariousness and beauty and utter persistence. This existence may be deeply flawed, but still, the moon moves the ocean, and a small, round globe spins on a fixed axis hurtling through space. And the taste of life, bitter and sweet and sharp, is better than any food I've ever known.

[8] C.S. Lewis, *The Problem of Pain*. Copyright © C.S. Lewis Pte. Ltd. 1940. Extract reprinted by permission.

SOUTH BEND, INDIANA

At five in the morning Finn wakes and dresses quickly. He has packed three outfits for the long weekend and now, on the fourth morning, is wearing some iteration of all three: baseball cap and jeans and a newly purchased leather jacket in the style of Indiana Jones over a white t-shirt. He paces the room eating sardines and Cheetos before the sun has even risen, and I think to myself, tired and happy and a little bewildered, *I like this man*. He pauses at the edge of the bed where I sit cross-legged and mostly naked and we eat jelly beans and laugh, drunk on only two hours of sleep.

Come with me, he says.

I have a job, I reply, laughing, smiling.

When he leaves he gathers his bags, his sunglasses already on. His eyes are gray and green and light and lovely, but in this moment there is something in them he doesn't want me to see, and I let him have this. We kiss as though it is just another day, as though we have not just met, as though we'll see each other soon, and often. He flies west, I go east. Suddenly I am dreaming of California and a boy with a shock of freckles across his nose.

★

He is a few paces away the first time I see him. I turn to my girlfriend Krysta and say, *That guy, there. Really?* she says, her eyebrows lifting in mild surprise. His face is half-obscured by a beard and I too am surprised I don't mind it. Krysta and I laugh quietly, happily; this weekend is a celebration—the sort that makes anything possible and everything light. He takes a step towards us to tell us we must take our seats, his body angling in, his tux perfectly cut. He is careful not to get too close; I note this.

Krysta and I walk around the back and slip into a pew, and the mass begins. At my request she kindly sits between me and a guy I kissed in a bar in New York a few months back—the last guy I kissed, actually. I remember I was wearing a tight black sweater and my hair was pulled into a high ponytail. I had on very little makeup but for the red on my lips, and I felt unusually beautiful. A girl in the bar stopped me on the way in to say so and I smiled and thanked her. But I was lonely. It was the end of April, New York was still chilly, and everything felt in-between, myself most of all.

I'd gone there with Elle to see Charles play with his band. They didn't go on until after midnight, which was just about the time I went to bed most nights, and when we arrived at eleven there was already a line wrapped around the building. I turned to Elle, my mouth open, a question half-formed. *Oh yeah, they are a thing,* she said laughing, clearly delighted. We'd all been living together for five months, and I didn't even know Charles played an instrument. For the two hours they played, a riot of music and joy spilling from the stage, I closed my eyes and swayed my hips and played at being fine. And I was, mostly, but for the part of me that wasn't—the part of me that was tired and lonely and half-stuck in a life I was only half-living, one foot in, one foot out.

After the band had finished and as we stood around in the too-small venue on Houston Street, Elle pulled the drummer towards me. She'd whispered in my ear as all the guys were still on stage that he was recently single and I'd smiled, my head nodding to the beat of the music. It was a clunky setup, and one I didn't really have the energy to untangle myself from. So I got drunk on two glasses of whiskey and as I leaned against the bar, and as he leaned in promising me that he had *quite the story*, I kissed him, for no reason other than I wanted to feel a man's hands on the small of my back. I am not proud of this, but loneliness is occasionally a wave that topples a person and leaves one standing on an unexpected shore-line gasping for air.

Charles, Elle, and I had finished the night eating corned beef sandwiches at five in the morning on the Lower East Side before sharing a cab home. The sun was just coming up over the Hudson when we turned the key in the door and silently fell into our respective beds. When, months later, Elle asked if I wanted to sit next to the drummer at her wedding reception, I politely declined with nothing more than a shake of my head and slight flush of my cheeks. I am startled to see him sitting in the pew, his eyes bluer than I had remembered, handsome in this light.

I don't think of the guy from the back of the church—the one in the tux—until we all sit down to dinner. He's at the next table over and I watch him during the speeches. I like how he has turned his body to listen, how he straddles the chair and throws his head back as he laughs—there is nothing self-conscious about the way he takes up space. It is just as dinner is ending that I catch his eye and hold it for longer than is comfortable or polite. I barely know who I am, I've spent whole years trying to work up the courage to look at some men this way. I watch him on the dance floor as he moves easily, his joy unmeasured and a little messy, the top button of his shirt undone, and I think again, *That guy*. When we finally get close on the dance floor, Krysta pulls me away, towards the cake, or something else not nearly as important and I laugh, *I was so close! Oh!* she says realizing her mistake. Later I push past him to get a drink and he nearly ducks to get out of the way; I take special pleasure in teasing him about this at the end of the night.

I'm not sure exactly how it happens, but suddenly we are in a larger group, and I stick out my hand and say hello and learn his name—Finn. I promptly proceed to talk about politics or something else wildly inappropriate for a wedding, which he is kind enough to point out, then asks me to dance anyway. When, in between spins and dips, I ask him where he has learned to dance so well, he tells me his father once pointed to a dance floor and said, *You see that, son? That's where the girls will be.* I clutch his hand tightly and he spins me again, pausing just long enough to kiss me, his beard soft against my chin. Anne Lamott once wrote: "Churches are good for prayer, but so are garages and cars and mountains and showers and dance floors."[9] His hands on my waist feel as close to rapture as anything I've ever known.

My feet are filthy, having discarded my heels early enough into the evening to be considered inappropriate, and the sheets on the bed are so white. He suggests a shower and it takes me a moment to realize he means together. We strip unceremoniously and let the water run over us as we kiss and chat about all of the basic things. His parents and my parents. His sister and my brother. Where we are from and what we do. What make us sad and what gets us out of bed in the morning. It is so easy and uncomplicated. We cover a lot of ground, quickly. There is barely a beat between wrapping ourselves in towels and the moment he takes me to bed.

When all is said and done he turns to me and says, *I've never done that before.*

Done what? I ask, totally unsure what he's about to say.

Had sex for the first time while just talking about life.

---

[9] Anne Lamott, *Plan B: Further Thoughts on Faith* (New York: Riverhead Books, 2005).

He falls asleep with his arms wrapped tightly around me and doesn't let go for the whole of the night, wriggly as I am. My hair is wet and matted, and the tops of my cheeks are stained with mascara, but I feel in that moment as beautiful as I ever have.

We spend the next day in a larger group, taking in a baseball game, early July light angling across the playing field. It is so fun. This man is so fun. He is goofy and funny and unfailingly kind. He tells me a story about his time in the army and being forced to trim the grass one blade at a time with only his fingers. He laughs as he tells it. *Isn't it so odd and cool?* he asks. And I am struck by the fact that time hasn't softened the memory or spun it into something better than it was, that even as it occurred he delighted in its strangeness—and hell if there isn't a lesson in this. When the other guys who are with us make a joke at someone's expense, Finn turns away, removing himself from the conversation. He buys me cheap wine in a plastic cup because he knows I don't like beer, and pulls Twizzlers from his pocket, the act of which may as well be my personal love language, and I think: *This guy.*

We take turns in the batting cage where I challenge him to a contest before I realize that he is one of those frustratingly adept people who is good at nearly everything he does or tries to do. The teenagers running the pitching machines declare that I have won, but that is because they are twenty and male, and I am a girl in a short skirt and wedged heels who made sure to smile at them when we walked in. The loser has to run through the fountain, but in the end we do it together, gripping tightly to one another's hands, because in this context, to have won or lost is beside the point. Wet and suddenly cold against the Indiana air, he passes me his jacket and I wear it for the rest of the night, running the bases barefoot, red dirt between my toes, happy.

When the night ends, later than it should and too many drinks in, a group of ten of us still at the bar, I catch his eye.

I'm going to go, I say.

Oh. Oh, we're going? he asks, which is quietly what I'd been hoping for.

We fall asleep side by side, whispering the worst of who we are into the dark hotel room, because we are both human and flawed and better for it. And because neither one of us is afraid of our own worst selves. But weddings are funny things—celebrations and so many people privately reconciling the lives they didn't get.

There is so much I want to remember. The first moment I see him. How we actually meet, how I stick out my hand and say hello. How as soon as he takes me in his arms I know I'm not going to leave them. That moment while dancing when a whole chunk of my hair comes off in one of his buttons, and how we both look at each other in shock before laughing. The first time he kisses me, the feel of his hair, sweaty, curling at the ends beneath my fingertips. How he pulls the hem of my dress down after spinning me because I am embarrassed that it has inched up. How I am tipsy, but never drunk. The way the photo booth is situated under a set of stairs, and how, when he pulls the black curtain closed behind us, alone for the first time, we each let out a deep breath. *Kiss her*, the people on the stairs above all cheer, startling us with their presence; how he then takes my face in his hands and gently kisses me, a suspended moment in the chaos. I want to know what those four square photos look like and where they are—we don't stick around long enough to find out. My guess is, the two of us, locking lips, are barely in the frame. I want to remember how when we lie in bed that night he says that if I hadn't come up to him, he never would have said hello. How I then tuck my head into his shoulder, my cheeks flushing red.

Come to Los Angeles, Finn says as he gathers his things before heading to the airport on Monday morning.

I have a book deadline, I say.

Vancouver then, you can write there.

When did I tell him I am a writer? And can I call myself that? I am six weeks away from having to turn in a manuscript, and the fear associated with it has been crippling me for months now. I don't say any of this in the moment—I don't know what I say, actually, but it is not yes, when yes is all I want to say. I don't say that I'm afraid that when I'm done putting words onto paper I won't actually have a book. And if I cannot write the book, what then? If I cannot write the book who am I? Am I a person worthy of affection? Of his affection? As if the two things have anything to do with one another.

Just before leaving, as he moves about the room collecting loose items, he stops and turns to me and says the loveliest things. He is direct in his language and clear, to the point that I think surely I have let something slip without realizing it, revealed some deep insecurity—how else did he know to say exactly what I needed to hear? It does not occur to me that these things could flow from him, unprompted, simply because they are true and so, necessary to say.

I do not know how to meet him in this place. I talk a good game, but intimacy does not come easily to me. So I look up at him from my seated position on the bed, wide-eyed and mostly mute. *Same*, I say.

Happiness demands its own sort of courage.

When Elle and Charles return from their honeymoon and briefly stop in New York before returning to the West Coast where they have just moved, I kick Charles out of the living room for a few minutes of uninterrupted girl talk. Elle wants to know the details, and as we hash it out and I reveal certain insecurities she laughs at me because didn't I see how Finn looked at me as we all sat watching fireworks after the baseball game?

What? I ask.

You know, she teases me.

Except that I don't. I have no memory of it. I remember her sitting in front of me, Charles, too, and I remember what they were wearing, but I have no memory of this man—this man I so immediately adored—sitting beside me. I tell her this.

Were you drunk? she asks, confused.

No. No, I wasn't.

I know exactly what happened before, and I know exactly what happened after, but what the hell is she talking about? We both sit in silence for a moment puzzling over this; I suspect she doesn't believe me. But it is as simple as I cannot remember watching the fireworks next to this man, my body nestled into his, and any half-memory of it is, at this point, imagined. I am fighting the hole in my memory and the deep fear from which it arises.

The night we met, lying in bed, Finn had said to me, *This is going to sound like a line* followed by something else I have no memory of. I don't know what it was. I don't know what he said. I have no idea what sounded like a line. It must have been good. Was it? And why can't I remember?

Finn promises to come to New York. But he takes so long to choose a date—too long. Charles tells me that he is a man of his word, that if he says he will come, then he will; I hang on to this. I finish painting my room and buy plants and an extra pillow, and I imagine what it will be to open the door to him when he arrives, to sit across from him at the restaurant around the corner. But he never comes. He never chooses a date. And he becomes one more man who fails to do the thing he says he will.

Months later I fly west to visit Charles and Elle in Los Angeles. Finn and I meet in a bar that first night. He lifts me into the air and we order drinks, and I can tell that we are both nervous, chatting breezily while staring at our hands, quietly feeling our way back to one another. Later we go bowling and he thinks I'm not trying, but I'm just really that bad at knocking down ten pins. We stay awake all night eating shitty fast food and discussing politics and virtual realities and where science meets faith. He kisses my shoulders and pulls me into him, tells me that he missed me, but the closer we become, the wider the gap grows—the more I know, the less is clear. There is a continent between us. I can tell by the way he looks at me—there is a hesitation that was not there before, a sadness, too. But then I wonder if he's simply mirroring the fear I feel.

I cannot tell you how I know he is not right, only that we both feel it.

Occasionally Finn smiles at me in a way that is goofy but put-on, and I want to tell him not to do that. That I like him best in the moments when he thinks no one is watching—when he is quiet and kind and perfectly himself, without pretense or the need to please. I want to whisper in his ear, in the dark, as we lie entwined that he is remarkable because of who he is, not what he is—and that should a part of his life change, he'd still be enough. More than, actually.

But just as it is not my job to convince a man to love me, it cannot be my job to convince a man that he is worthy of the love that I have to offer.

Days later I stand in a doorway for the second time as he walks away from me. This time he barely says goodbye, kissing me quickly. *I'll see you*, I say, the words trailing off. He doesn't turn around to look back at me and I don't blame him. It is a different kind of goodbye this time and we both feel it. I watch as he walks away and I close the door, a pang of loneliness catching in my chest, one that I am sure will pass.

ON HOME, III

Meet me in the place beyond failure. In the heart-break and humility of a shitty hand of cards. Tell me about the thing you did exactly right that didn't work, and how you learned that control is an illusion. Because sometimes a child hits his head on the kitchen counter and has to be rushed to the hospital, blood on the back-seat, and it's no one's fault. Because life is neither tidy, nor fair: cancer coming just two months after a wedding. Tell me you know—really know—that there is no way to protect against heartache, and so you won't even try.

Point to the line in the sand, and say, *This is the thing that split my world into a Before and an After, and this is how I carried on.* Take my hand and remind me that there is joy even in what is broken.

Because all I really want to know is that you are kind and good and whole—that you have suffered sadness, but no longer wear it. That you'll cup the back of my neck and kiss me hard and ask me to dance on the sub-way platform, to hell with anyone who might see. That you'll show up, even when showing up isn't convenient or easy, and carries no guarantees. That you'll get on the plane and meet me at my door and hoist me into the air because you gave me your word. That, despite your fears and frustrations, you'll show up—honestly and stripped of bravado and the need to impress. Because when everything else falls away, this is how we will love each other. Simply and quietly, with a held hand, a long kiss, a quiet understanding, in that place beyond failure, where we meet fear with hope.

PARIS

*"Paris was always worth it and you received
return for whatever you brought to it."*
Ernest Hemingway, *A Moveable Feast*

My mother and I go to Paris two years after I am meant to go with Eric. We fly late on a Friday night after eating burgers and fries and drinking cheap wine in the airport café. We stay on an island on the Seine in the middle of the city, and for the first three days I stare at the river and I stare at the buildings and I feel as though I can't really see any of it. There is music and dancing and the sublime cadence of the French tongue, and the city is beautiful in a way I barely have words for. But I am three feet behind myself, the images refusing to press themselves against my eyes; I am afraid I am missing my life, and I don't know how to say this out loud.

The first afternoon we sit along the bank of the Seine and eat pungent cheeses with plastic knives, our fingers tearing into a single baguette, bottles of sparkling water between us. There is a small band of folk musicians a hundred feet away, and a large group has gathered to sing and clap. For as long as I live, I shall remember this moment for how happy I am and how much I love my mother and how large the world seems. And for the feeling of my own heart breaking because I cannot freeze time.

We spend hours wandering the Tuileries Garden. Through the Arc de Triomphe du Carrousel, past the small ponds around which people lounge in green chairs reading and smoking and soaking in the sun. We settle finally on a small square of grass, flanked on all sides by tall, perfectly hedged trees. I lie down, close my eyes, and listen. I want to remember this. The sound of my mother folding and unfolding the map. Children squealing as they chase a dog a hundred feet away who in a moment will sniff the spot where my hair meets my neck.

That night we find a small café in Le Marais and drink wine and eat *steak frites*, the couple at the table next to us listening in on our conversation. After dinner we fall asleep quickly, waking only once—just as the sun is rising and a young man, finding his way home, snakes his way through the narrow streets, singing at the top of his lungs, a bottle in hand. The sky is a hazy gray and I climb out of bed to close the window, muting his one-man parade.

Over the next few days we take Communion in Notre-Dame and light a candle for my grandmother. We wander up the long, ivy-covered alley to see where James

Joyce lived and wrote *Ulysses*. I photograph everything, a large camera between my hands, the weighty lens tangible in a way few things are. We eat oranges in Rodin's garden and duck into open entryways when the rain becomes unmanageable. We find the apartments of Hemingway and Fitzgerald and then sit outside of Les Deux Magots eating boiled peanuts and drinking white wine.

It is May, but Paris is unseasonably wet and cold. All over the city museums are preparing for the floods by moving items in storage to higher ground. I buy small black boots and wear them out of the department store, my ballet flats soaked, and my mother and I wrap scarves around our necks, wishing occasionally for warmer coats. The Seine floods the week after we leave.

We walk everywhere, always returning to the tiny island in the middle of the city. Each day, we march past the Louvre and the Tuileries Garden, past the Pont des Arts and Pont Neuf, the Seine on our right and the small green stalls that line it overflowing with prints and books. On the third day we visit the Musée d'Orsay where we see works by Manet and Monet and Van Gogh's *Starry Night Over the Rhone*. It is so beautiful that it seems to glow from within. Standing in front of it, I begin to cry because I've never seen anything like it, and because 200 years ago a man by the name of Vincent wrote in a letter to his brother:

> *What I am in the eyes of most people—a nonentity, an eccen-*
> *tric, or an unpleasant person—somebody who has no position in*

society and will never have; in short, the lowest of the low. All
right, then—even if that were absolutely true, then I should like
to show by my work what such an eccentric, such a nobody, has
in his heart.[10]

He then set brush to canvas and made this thing—this
perfect, incredible, indelible thing—that in a dark
museum hundreds of years later group after group after
group will gather in front of in silent awe. He was a man
who surely wrestled with the fear that he was not enough.
And who from a blank canvas wrested the divine.

I cry standing in front of it because beauty and love
are their own dark arts, and humanity never ceases to
surprise me.

Hours later I take the Metro across the city. I am late
to meet my friend Laura, and I am breathless and a little embarrassed. Tardiness is a quality I abhor in others,
but the tour of the Musee d'Orsay had been long, and
Van Gogh's *The Starry Night* was one of the most beautiful
things I'd ever seen, and there are so many steps up to
the Basilica. Two years of emails back and forth, and here
we are, meeting, finally, in the corner of a French café
with plastic tablecloths, that smells suspiciously like piss.

Laura had sent me an email some years ago that I
have no memory of. And then sent another when we

[10] Vincent Van Gogh, Ronald de Leeuw (ed.) & Arnold Pomerans
(trans.), *The Letters of Vincent Van Gogh* (London: Penguin, 1997).

were both 28. That email led to a near daily exchange, the promise of her words a daily salve during a time in my life when heartache felt more immediate than not. In this small Parisian café, we begin our conversation where our last note left off. We order two glasses of rosé and a cheese plate, and then settle back into our chairs.

For the first time since getting off the plane I begin to breathe, the middle of my chest softening, my spine suddenly firm and rooted. I am seated in a chair in Paris across from a person I adore—this person to whom I have written for two years, who knows all of my secrets, who knows of Jack and Caroline and Will and my frustrations with New York, who knows how stuck I feel in my own life. We talk about loss and grief and all of the things in between. We lay our lives bare on that table, discussing what we are willing to sacrifice, and those points on which we will not compromise. Then we order two more glasses of rosé and I spoon spicy mustard onto bits of bread, and Laura asks me what it is like to see Paris after all of this time, and I, barely meeting her eyes, tell her that I'm only just now catching up to myself.

We leave the café and wander the narrow streets, stopping into vintage clothing shops and posing in front of chic Parisian restaurants, laughing as we try on this other life, as though it's as easy to slip into as one of the dresses we've just marveled at. We take a cab across the city to see my mother, and there's something about the speed of the car, the city zooming past, and Laura next to me—I am so happy and struck by just how simple and quiet a feeling it is. Blink and you'll miss it.

Two weeks later I return to New York and sit at a small desk, at a job that I hate, and I think of Van Gogh and Laura and my mother and Hemingway and Fitzgerald, and of the improbable beauty of Paris.

As I ride the subway to work in the mornings, passing through the turnstiles and standing on the crowded train jockeying for space, I feel my life retreating like a wave at low tide, returning only as I venture back uptown in the evening.

When people ask about Paris, if it was *worth the wait*, I smile and nod and say, *Yes, yes, of course.* When what I'm really thinking is: *I am wasting my life.* Every day someone stands in front of a painting and is moved by grace. Every day someone walks along the Seine. Every night people dine on bread and cheese and wine and steak. Not every person, and not all the time, but there is so much beauty in the world and I am wasting my life just making it through the day. I have wrongly assumed that in making myself small, in settling for a job I hate, other things will be easier. It will be easier to meet a man and buy a house and get the proverbial white picket fence. I am treading water in my own life until I can slip into someone else's. I'm not waiting for the subway, I'm waiting for the man. *Oh God*, I think, shame rising unbidden at the realization.

And so I quit my job. Because life is too short and too good to miss. And because it must belong to me before

I can choose to share it with anyone else. I fly west, and as the plane takes off, I feel—for the first time in as long as I can remember—like my life is my own. People will tell you that you cannot live in the past. But when your life is built on a thousand and one small concessions you have made because things did not go as planned, then life itself is three feet behind you. When you seek out stability for fear of failure, you have already lost.

Our job is not to create a masterpiece, but to give voice to that which only we can give voice to. Our job is to go to work doing that which we feel called to do. Despite our fears—despite the nagging notion that we are not enough, or too much, or fraudulent, we show up. We take risks. We wrestle with our wants and our needs and the blank canvas. And we let the wrestling change us. Because in the space of that change—in the space of who we once were and who we become—is the divine. Everything else is a trick of the light. Sometimes in wrestling with the blank canvas we get a *Starry Night*, and sometimes all we get are the honest, imperfect words that this writer offers up because they are all she has, and so worthy by that measure alone.

And so yes, Paris was worth the wait.

NEW YORK

Sometimes I think of how I will describe New York to my children.

I will tell them the smell of Magnolia Bakery was that of loneliness. That I spent too many mornings getting off the D train at 50th en route to a job that was never—not once—good. I will say that I used to cover my nose as I left the station just to avoid the scent of the bakery above; it felt out of place for the hour, and I felt out of place in my life. But I will tell them that it was my becoming.

I will pull out a map and point to a small stretch of Columbus Avenue on which, aged nineteen, at two in the morning, I hurled snowballs at friends in the middle of a February snowstorm. I will say that running down the wide, empty avenue with packed snow between my hands felt joyous and messy and heartbreakingly transient.

I will say that at a pizza dive on 71st Street after our first-year Discovery project—a rite of passage for Juilliard students—a classmate put his hand on my knee beneath the table. There were six of us sitting in the small booth, and I didn't know how to tell him that I was in love with the boy just to his right.

I will tell them that eventually I was flanked by women who were wildly intelligent. Women who spoke their minds and offered kindness, who overflowed with opinions and ideas and the belief that they deserved to take up space in the world. I will tell them that there are few things I am prouder of than the women I met in New York—fierce, fiery women who made space for sorrow, who gave voice to their fears, and who carved out success on their own terms.

I will say that at 29 I went to a Jesuit church on 16th Street. The girl in the pew in front of me cried quietly, the priest said his first mass, and the whole of the congregation clapped, and I thought, *If God is only ever an idea, that is enough.*

I will explain that when I lived in an apartment on Thompson Street, between Christopher and West Houston, I would watch as men in fine linens ferried bottles of wine between a windowless restaurant and an unmarked apartment. And their quiet parade was the very best thing about that very terrible year of my life.

And I will tell them how I once watched a man on the C train play a scratch-off lottery ticket and my heart broke for the hope in that small action.

I will say that, for me, New York was a city halved in two: East and West; lonely and less so.

And that once upon a time the route to a job that I couldn't stand took me east on 53rd, where often I'd see the same man walk his little girl from the lobby of their building to a bus just outside. He was slightly older than I imagined the fathers of most ten year olds to be, and it seemed she had different challenges than most children, but I was always struck by their joy, by the levity with which they carried their load. By their wide smiles and her hand in his. And how whenever I saw them I'd send up a small prayer of thanks and think, *Okay, so it can all be a little bit lighter.*

And that at the age of 30 I stood on the corner of 119th and Manhattan, as a person I cared for told me he hated me. We were tethered in a way that could not be broken by such words, and so I stood with my hand on his arm, and I listened. This was my gift to him. This was all I could think to do—to stand in the truth and the hurt of that beside him. It would have broken my heart, except that there was something about the sound of it that caught my ear, and so I followed his thought home: *I hate you. I hate how you make me feel. I hate this feeling.* Which was heartbreaking in a different way from being hated because we cannot solve that discomfort for another person. We can only wave to them from the shoreline of having survived that particular journey and tell them that those waves won't always threaten to sink the ship. Eventually you learn to swim and it's never so scary again.

I will tell them that the city was, in so many ways, and for such a long time, the best and worst thing about my life. That it was a perpetual question in pursuit of an answer. And that in attempting to answer it, I turned and faced myself. And how once I did, there was no going back.

119TH AND
FREDRICK DOUGLASS BOULEVARD

We sit across from one another, a small table between us, coats and bags at our feet. It is cold out and the requisite clothing, now off, is spilling over towards the next table. I sip on a glass of white wine. David tells me it's not good for me. He drinks water. *Carbs too*, he says. He orders meat; I ask for the pasta.

We stopped dating some years before and forged an uncomfortable friendship built on hard questions and spontaneous dinners. He has met someone. She is blonde and successful, and will never know my name. I have not met someone, so he asks, *What will you bring to the table?*

Me. I'll bring me, I say, a little incredulous.

You have an awfully high opinion of yourself, David says, smiling as he settles back into his chair, which would be insulting, if it wasn't just further confirmation of how ill-suited we were.

It isn't a business deal, I want to say.

Do you love her? I ask. He gives me a small smile and sidesteps the question. I ask him if he doesn't think he should hold out for the real thing? He laughs. David thinks my version of the real thing is nonsense—non-existent. And we sit there without speaking, wondering who is right. And living with the possibility that, in this context, *right* is beside the point.

But it is for this reason—and so many others—that our affection begins and ends with dinners and hard questions and a kiss goodnight. And with him walking away.

So I drink my wine. Because I believe in a glass with dinner. And I order the pasta, because I believe in carbs, too. And I let him kiss my cheek, and I tug on the collar of his coat, and then I go home and I write.

And I sit with my questions and my fear and all the damn uncertainty.

It is a humbling thing to watch people around you build a life with a person when their love feels like an approximation, a shadow thing—Plato's Cave, where one mistakes cutouts for the real thing. It is humbling because you are the beneficiary of their failures—what you want and what you need made ever clearer. A study in contrasts.

I do not know much, but this is what I believe: Love is not a frenzied, desperate act. It is not a thing that bestows worth upon a person. The worth must come first, mined mostly on one's own.

At eighteen I fell in love with a man I will never speak ill of. Will was blazingly smart and wickedly talented, but he was not my guy. It took me years to understand this: not my guy and not my life. I may not love him anymore, but goodness am I thankful for him. Because the thing about falling in love at eighteen and being able to say, so many years later, *Yes, it was love*, is that it creates a specific point of reference—a baseline of what to expect and what to demand, an understanding of what the whole damn mess feels like—which means I'll never be 33, asking the person across the table what they bring to it.

Recently I dreamt about Jack. He held a baby in his arms; it wasn't his baby and it wasn't mine. But for that afternoon, the child was in my charge, and seeing a baby in his arms was magic. He cradled it so carefully, was giddy with affection. But someone walked into the room and told him he had to go, that he didn't belong. I countered, *No, no. He's here for me. He's here because I want him here. And he's so good with the baby—can't you see?* But he was told he had to go; and so he did.

I awoke the next morning both startled and tremendously at peace. The dream felt telling. Because it wasn't really about Jack; it was about the room, and the fact that I was in it. You see, I think that room was love and All Good Things That Are Still to Come. It was an ever-after. And I was there, feet firmly planted. Because I have looked the worst parts of myself in the eye and either changed them or made peace with them. Because I finally feel worthy of love, even at this imperfect moment in my life—when people still ask what I'm bringing to the table. And if I am worthy of love now, then I am worthy of love always. I have faith in all that is yet to come.

Jack didn't have to leave. He only *thought* he did. That's what struck me about the dream—that we enter and leave that room only by our own consent. And the battle for one's worth is a mostly private one.

We don't talk about that much, do we? How we have to fight for ourselves and care for ourselves, and ultimately *face* ourselves? How the best and most courageous and most compelling thing we can do is cultivate self-love. How it's not some New Age prophecy, but a very real and very necessary investment. How self-love is the source of empathy and honesty and love of a partner, if that's your thing.

The best people I know are comfortable with failure, willing to hang out in discomfort. They aren't interested in looking cool or terribly concerned with fitting in. They understand the value of listening and are willing to apologize and admit wrong. They are engaged in the very active thing that is fighting for the life you want, and fighting for the love you think you deserve. And at the end of the day, when asked what they bring to the table, they know the answer.

HUDSON STREET

I flew to Chicago last August because I thought, *If not New York, somewhere else*. I rode a bike along Lake Shore Drive and visited friends, ate popsicles on the beach, and drank very expensive wine on the rooftop of the Athletic Club. But it didn't feel quite right. Or, well, I didn't.

Joni told me I had to figure out a way to make peace with New York.

No, no, I just don't like it, I said, sitting at the kitchen table. *It's no more complicated than that*.

And she smiled at me, sipping the drink in front of her. *Yeah, I get that, I really do. But still*, she said, letting the words trail off.

Three weeks before turning 30, walking north on Hudson Street on a Saturday morning, coffee in hand, the city cool and light, something shifted, a corner was turned. I saw New York through new eyes and I saw myself as a woman changed—so different from the girl who arrived here at eighteen. So unlike the young woman who rode the A train with Will, or smoked a single cigar on a sloping hill in Central Park.

I'll never forget how, at the age of twenty, I sat in my tiny dorm room at Juilliard and sadness crept in for the first time. Thank God I didn't know all that was to come. It was there that a desperate hunger took hold, one that would take me years to understand as a pursuit of home—a desperate search for meaning. The twenties are hard. Everyone who is not in their twenties says this. And everyone who is in their twenties *knows* this. But when you are in the middle of it, hearing people who are not, say, *Yeah, it's rough*, isn't terribly helpful. But then you start to crest upon a new decade and you think, *Holy shit! The twenties are so, so, hard, but the view from up here is incredible!*

I have never felt more beautiful than I did when I turned 30. I have never felt smarter. I have never felt more valuable. I have never been so sure of what I have to offer. I have never been so at peace with my body, so safe in my own skin. I have never cared less for what people I don't care about think of me. Everything feels lighter, easier. What was never personal is—for the first time—*actually not personal*.

But I think, more than anything, the real gift of a new decade is this: I'm no longer afraid of what comes next (or doesn't). In so many ways my twenties were defined by a fear of the future—a fear that the future wouldn't exist to me. Not that time would stop, but that nothing would ever change; that good things were, quite literally, impossible. I didn't trust the persistence and inevitably of time.

Three weeks from 30, walking along the westernmost edge of the city, I looked around at the innumerable blessings in my life and I marveled at their ability to multiply. Good things *do* happen. And very often the things we fear the most are not only bearable, but transformative. We will all, many times over, have to reconcile the life we planned for with the life we've got.

There is not one thing I wish I had learned sooner. There is not one thing I think I was meant to know before I knew it. Because I learned about trusting my gut only after I didn't. And I learned about love in the trenches of heartbreak. And I understood the value of showing up only after I failed to do so. But it is how I learned each thing that has shaped the woman I am today, and the woman I'll be tomorrow, and the day after.

ON HOME, IV

I've begun to dream in sounds. The hiss and spit of the coffee pot. The swish, thump of the washing machine. The low hum of a television in the background. The creak of the floor beneath my feet. The front door as it opens and closes. Laughter. Someone running water. The rustle of the newspaper as it is folded and smoothed. The thud of your mug against the table. The tap of your fingers. My own deep and thankful breath. The single pop of the toaster. The scrape of your chair as it pushes back. Small footsteps.

I am sitting at a table, in the kitchen, the window open, a breeze slipping in, morning light angling across the book in front of me, and I am surrounded by the quiet symphony of our everyday life. There are no words for my love for you. There is only the sound of my lips on the back of your neck and the soft thud of your keys on the hall table. And suddenly home is not a place, but the inhalation and exhalation of your breath as you sleep in bed beside me.

MANHATTAN AVENUE

I return to New York after a month away and walk the five blocks from the train to the brownstone. The city in autumn is equal parts explosion and bouquet. It is profusion of light. It is the soft, gray glow of late afternoons, cool weather creeping in. The trees are losing their leaves, finally. I breathe in the crisp air, the scent of a fire in the distance. Sometimes I think if the only joy of leaving home is the gift of returning to it, then that is enough. But on this occasion, walking those five blocks towards the brownstone, I am both deeply content and wildly homesick and I wonder how both of these things can be true.

In my first year at Juilliard we took a class in which we learned the basics of music comprehension. I remember sitting in the small classroom and the professor pointing out how *directional* the music was—and then asking us to use one ear to listen in one direction—to follow the melody, and our other ear to listen to the bassline. It was maddeningly difficult, and I felt like I failed at it more often than not. And yet, I think of it often. How one piece—a song, a movement, a symphony—is made up of many parts, all moving in different directions, all working together to create something layered and whole.

More than one thing can be true at the same time.

I have spent the last decade or so in search of home—the place, the person, the meaning of the word. The French have no word for home. They have words for "at my place" and "in my country," but not for "home," which is far more ambiguous, and I can't help but think they are on to something. For thirteen years I have been scything the tall grasses that I felt sure obscured it, gripping tightly to the handle and grasping at anything that looked the part, secretly a little desperate for another person to guide me there. And only now am I realizing that home is like anything important—it cannot be contained or circumscribed; it is within and without. It is larger than language allows for.

As I walk past the brownstones lining this southern part of Harlem, past the grocery store and the school and the park, the last of the leaves now fire-engine red, my heart aches for the friends I have just left behind in California, for my parents in Texas, for the mountains of Utah now surely white with snow. Home is so much larger than this tiny corner of Manhattan. And yet, it wasn't always what it is now. And it may never again be what it is in this moment.

I pause on the corner of Manhattan Avenue and 121st Street, and I study how the light cuts into the red brick across the street. I watch as an older couple passes me on their way to Morningside Park. And then I gather my bags and climb the nine steps before pushing the door open. Home, finally.

ON HOME, V

I am every story I have ever read. And every word I have ever written. I am every song that has made me go quiet. I am thirteen years of loneliness in this city, and the desire to leave it. I am the girl who wants to go to Morocco and Prague, Barcelona and Berlin. Who occasionally brings her wine glass into the shower. I am quiet mornings and endless lattes and long road trips, my fingers dragging in the breeze out the open window. I am the six years of counting calories and the three years I have no memory of. I am the sadness that nearly swallowed me whole, and I am the stumbling, stubborn journey back from its mouth. I am every man who has hurt me, and the quiet hope that we've only got to get it right once. And I am the belief that life, as it is right now, is enough—more than enough, actually. I am loved, and I love, and home is everywhere I look.

93RD AND MADISON

He wakes early for work and I listen from bed as he showers quickly. His feet on the floor, the hangers in the hall closet rattling gently as he reaches for a button-down. *I'm late*, Harry says appearing in the doorway, his blond hair still wet, his fingers making quick work of the buttons as he bends down to kiss me.

This is goodbye, but neither of us says it. I am a week away from leaving New York—headed south to a small town along the Eastern Seaboard where I will spend my days in classrooms attending lectures and writing papers in gray stone buildings. He is leaving three days later, flying home to London, his yearlong postdoc fellowship nearly done. I get out of bed a few minutes after he leaves, collecting the water glasses on the nightstand, making the bed, tidying up a little, but careful not to cross the line of too-much. I shower and dress and scribble a note that I leave on the fridge—one that will take him a week to find. And then I leave, closing the door behind me, turning the knob to make sure the lock has caught. I stand there for a moment, aware that the world behind that door is now lost to me.

I walk west across the top of the park and for a moment allow myself to imagine another version of this life. One in which Harry and I live in his too-small apartment on the Upper East Side, and he goes to work each morning and comes home each night, and I never once take for granted the scent of coffee in the morning signaling that he is up before me. One in which he loves me as much as I love him.

For the few months leading up to my departure, friends ask if I am ready to leave, and I smile and pause and sidestep the question. Because the truth is, I am. I am ready to leave New York—I just don't want to leave this man.

I met Harry in a snowstorm and liked him right away. He loved his family. Called his father a legend. Adored his two older brothers. Spoke with awe and humor when referring to his mother. He worked impossible hours, slept too little, and I perpetually worried he wasn't eating enough. But sitting on his couch, stealing ten minutes before the day began, drinking coffee from his small stovetop espresso maker, I thought, *I could do this forever.*

When you have been alone longer than most, there are certain things you learn. Chief among them is this: there is no one person for you. The world is wide and vast, and sometimes you meet the right person at the wrong time.

I closed the door to his apartment on the Wednesday morning the week before I left New York aware that I was losing not just this man, but my own dream for what I thought New York was supposed to be.

Everything that happened here was both okay and not—and only now that the worst has passed can I say that. Only now, just before I go, can I say it was fine because it had to be, but it also wasn't. It was really hard. There will come a day, in the not so distant future, when I will forget what it felt like to have people ask what I am doing with my life and not have an answer. I will forget the helplessness I felt sitting at dinner tables being asked, albeit subtly, to defend my worth and my time and my life. When I alone was not enough.

Everything has changed, and nothing has. Everything will be different, and nothing will.

I moved here at eighteen, and I've never known a day of my adult life anywhere else. I've come to learn that when you tell people you are leaving New York, they cock their head and get this very particular look on their face. Their response has almost nothing to do with you, and everything to do with them. New York: the great *What if* for so many—an idea, and not a city.

People have told me that there is almost no way to prepare for how beautiful a place becomes just before you go, made sweet by its impermanence. I walk home through the park, the July air sticky and thick, everything green, a certain light catching the corner of my eye, tears rolling down my cheeks, and I think, *I could have loved this place; perhaps I already do.*

YOU ARE HERE

This is what I now know. This is the cumulative knowledge of my twenties:

Give yourself permission to not be good at something. To write messy and imperfect words. To kiss a boy in the bar for no reason other than you want to. To let your legs shake during yoga. Stop apologizing for your height, for wanting to wear heels, for the actual space you take up in the world. Stand up straight. Uncross your arms. Regard as much as you can with awe.

Make lists of tangible things for when you need something to hang on to:

1. Wash the sheets.
2. Wipe the counter.
3. Grind the coffee beans.
4. Knead the bread.

Carve out a life on your own terms. Say *Thank you* and *I love you* and *I'm sorry*. "Heave your heart into your mouth."[11]

---

[11] To borrow from Shakespeare. In *King Lear*, Act I, Scene I, Cordelia says, "Unhappy that I am, I cannot heave my heart into my mouth."

Try new things. Reinvent. Try again. Show up. Celebrate the small successes. Make sure your identity isn't based on something you might lose. You are not the size of your waist or your health or your job or someone else's opinion of you. You are not the worst thing that has ever happened to you, and you are not the best, either.

Forgive yourself the moments you cannot remember; you were mining something sacred in that darkness. Forgive the half loaf of banana bread you ate on the train one night just to keep from falling asleep. Forgive the bathrooms you hid in crying, the thought of facing the world outside harder than you cared to admit.

Move your body more. Be generous in how you care for it, but not rigid. Stretch. Breathe into downward dog. Keep a valid passport. Do the hard things. Adapt. Admit fault. Take more risks. Bigger risks. Allow yourself to want more. Hold fast to hope. Wear heavy eyeliner and light sweaters and tight pants and flirt when you want to. Figure out what you believe in. Criticize only insofar as you are invested in helping the person change. Go to Paris; saber the champagne. Reframe your idea of failure. Learn to meditate. Pray—when it's hard, when it's uncomfortable, on the subway or walking home, offer up small and imperfect words because, in ways that are not wholly clear to you, they are important. Make sure the first two words are always *Thank you*.

Know that to want a life bigger than sadness is to accept a life in which sadness plays a part.

The thing about life being really shitty for a really long time is this: it gets better. Because the happiness that follows sadness is never the same as that which came before it. Shame recedes like the waves at low tide, and gratitude rushes in. For everything. For the whole of your life. Not a part of it, but the whole messy lot. And for the grace that is that mess. The perfect ordered chaos of it.

Everything worthy and good I learned through the lens of an unrelenting, impossible sadness. And I wouldn't have had it any other way.

Euphoros, from which we derive the term "euphoria," means "the bearer of goodness"—figure out how to be that for others. When you're feeling blue, hook into kindness. That way lies something far more urgent and important than happiness. Keep going, not because it's easy, but because that is what it is to be human—to continuously show up despite the fact that it's hard. You are not the first person to feel afraid, and you are not the first person to feel unworthy, but that is where your story begins, not where it ends. There is no roadmap. There is only faith. The act of it, if not the feeling.

Keep going.

ST. PATRICK'S CATHEDRAL

I sat in church this morning. Felt the wooden bench behind my knees and beneath my fingers. It was a stolen moment. A few minutes before the day began. I knelt and said a few words just as quietly as I could before leaning back and breathing. Someone once asked Teresa of Avila what she did during prayer and she said, "I just allow myself to be loved."

I have worn a long, gold pendant around my neck for nearly two years. I got it just after the start of a shitty job, after the heartache of Jack and the betrayal of Caroline. I got it when New York felt untenable, when everything was hard and I couldn't remember the taste or the feeling of hope. On it is the image of Ganesh, a Hindu deity known as the remover of obstacles, the patron of arts and sciences, and the god of beginnings.

The Catholic in me is well versed in the notion that help comes in many forms, and so I don't think it odd that a Hindu god sits flush against my chest, close to my heart. And I don't believe in a God whose sense of self is so tenuous that he would be offended by such a thing. A girlfriend who was raised practicing Hinduism looked at this pendant one morning and said to me, *You know the thing about Eastern religion—the difference between it and the Western canon—is that we don't believe that there will ever come a day when evil will be vanquished from the world. We believe in the coexistence of light and dark, good and evil.*

I knelt in church this morning thinking about how happiness and sadness are twin strands of the same thread. I thought about this odd and magic time in my life when everything is still unsettled and unknown, when I drink coffee in the evening and fight exhaustion in the day, when I am little sad, and a little not, but deeply sated—when my life is finally my own.

And then I leaned back, and let myself be loved.

THANKS

To my agent, Ella Kahn, who believed there was a book in me and generously waited while I unearthed it. To my editor, Kiera Jamison who, with unflinching precision, took that book and made it into this. Which is to say, better. To everyone at Icon for saying yes to my small collection of essays. To Claire Maxwell who sent the small message via Twitter that started it all. And to Laura Jane Williams who forged a path and then emailed me like a woman possessed to make sure I knew to follow.

RESOURCES

If you are struggling with an eating disorder then first let me say, I'm so sorry. It is torturous and rough, and very few people will ever understand it. If you are able to find a therapist who specializes in such an illness, see them. This is my best and most vociferous suggestion. If that is not feasible because the cost is prohibitive or mental health services are not valued or any of a hundred other reasons, then I humbly offer up the following:

Read *Appetites* by Caroline Knapp. New York: Counterpoint, 2003.

Listen to episode #589 of *This American Life*, "Tell Me I'm Fat," June 17, 2016: *www.thisamericanlife.org/radio-archives/episode/589/tell-me-im-fat*.

Then read *Shrill*. Lindy West writes about beauty and bodies and our own prejudices as few others do. New York: Hachette Books, 2016.

Google "The Great Starvation Experiment." or check out this piece about it on *Refinery29*, written by Kelsey Miller: "The Starvation Study That Changed The World", March 14, 2016, *www.refinery29.com/minnesota-starvation-experiment*.

Dig into the work that Lindsay and Lexi Kite are doing for *Beauty Redefined*: *beautyredefined.org*.

Give up "Fat Talk" for a week. And then for a second week. Don't look back. Check out "Tri Delta – Fat Talk Free Week" on YouTube: *https://youtu.be/KjqqVbcwpbM*.